20
THINGS
EVERY
"MOTIVATED"
20–SOMETHING
SHOULD
KNOW

Pavlina Osta

pavlinaosta@gmail.com

ISBN: 978-1-951503-15-4 (Ebook)
ISBN: 978-1-951503-14-7 (Paperback)

Published by Authorsunite.com

Table of Contents

FOREWORD

There's no substitute for experience. It is what makes you a better person, a better leader, and better at your profession of choice. No one knows everything in their twenties, or thirties or forties for that matter. Just because you have reached the pinnacle of success—whether the corner office at the c-suite or the highest title in the company—it doesn't mean you stop learning. Anyone who thinks they have stopped learning because they're successful is someone you need to run away from. Why? Because they're lying to themselves and they'll lie to you.

As an up-and-coming professional, you need to be a sponge—absorb as much knowledge as possible and apply it to your own experience. Here's what no one tells you: Advice doesn't have to come from someone older than you. It can come from anyone who has lived through any experience you haven't. Sometimes young professionals encounter a number of scenarios more seasoned executives have yet to delve into. Therefore, they become the experts and can teach US a few tricks that make our jobs (and sometimes life) easier.

Many people often say, "Oh, the ignorance of youth." And that may be true in some cases; however, what some tend to forget is how millennials and Gen Zers are more adaptable to change. They're malleable and can pivot quicker and with less disruptions than their older counterparts. That is your advantage. You're nimble, agile, and are more open to try new things and new processes—especially if it makes their work environment smoother and more engaged. I've always said, *work smarter, not harder,* and that's an adage we can all apply to ourselves today, tomorrow, and always.

Throughout the book, Pavlina adds a great deal of advice and best practices from a number of pretty successful people. And, as someone who has bought and sold over 250 businesses, someone who has been the CMO of a Fortune 100 company, and someone who is also an entrepreneur, here's my two cents:

> ➤ Ignore the naysayers, but learn how to differentiate constructive criticism from noise.
> ➤ Listen to everyone around you (young and old alike).
> ➤ Be objective.
> ➤ Put those nuggets of information into practice.

Remember, *if you ponder, you squander.* Get engaged, don't just have a plan A, plan B, or plan C. Have many plans because the unexpected will happen. A good leader is someone who is ready for any eventuality. And remember, an idea without implementation is just air—have a plan and execute on that plan. That's how you get ahead. Oh, and read the book, too.

Jeffrey Hayzlett – Primetime TV & Podcast Host, Chairman & CEO C-Suite Network, Keynote Speaker, Best-Selling Author and Global Business Celebrity

CHAPTER 1

Age is Not Your Excuse, It's Your Advantage!

"I think it's great that you're doing this, by the way. Like you, starting off now at 14 years old and, by the time you're 18 years old, you'll have a top journalism job. And, there will be people leaving your school at 18 years old, going to college coming out 22 years old, then starting at the bottom of some publication. So, it's really, really good you're doing this. So, keep it up."

~ Ed Sheeran, singer/songwriter ~
(from Ed Sheeran Interview with Pavlina 2012)

It was the 2012 Presidential elections. I approached the media check-in line, loaded down with camera gear, and gave the volunteers my name while handing them my ID. The high-security venue was for Republican candidate Mitt Romney. Seeing as he was the golden boy and popular in Florida, the venue was packed, despite the scorching heat and suffocating humidity.

Generally, there's a media entrance where one can be dropped off for a short walk to the venue. However, this event had me lugging camera gear up a grassy hill as I weaved through a couple thousand people. When the two elderly volunteers at the check-in table informed me I was not on the media list, I impatiently shoved my heavy camera gear back on my shoulders and requested they check again.

I wasn't in a polite mood. My voice carried in the hot, windless air when I was interviewing Romney and covering the event. It was so loud, in fact, that it caused security to do a double-take and move in closer.

The ladies searched through papers and shook their heads in confusion. Others at the table were getting flustered from the heat. It was then that I decided to take matters into my own hands. I addressed the closest security, "I need to get a seat with the media. Where's that at?"

Two security agents left their stations, escorted me through the metal detectors, and seated me in the front row of the stage, which was the area assigned to media and VIP guests.

I learned two things that day. Believe in yourself and size up the area to laser-in on who's ultimately in charge of what you want to accomplish.

With all the times we are told "no" or "you're not old enough," is it any wonder why we stop being assertive when we reach our teen years? Or even before that, actually, for girls! Studies have shown girls actually start self-doubting their own intelligence at the age of six! They begin thinking they're not as smart as boys. According to a study by famed researcher and associate professor at Cornell University, Lin Bian, this self-doubting continues throughout the lives of many girls! Girls apologize more, and they go through life thinking assertiveness is another word for "bitchy." Girls have been led not to think for themselves and, continuing into the twenty-first century, of not demanding equality and equity of themselves and their own worth.

Gender inequality is rampant, but just as strong in the inequality stakes is age inequality. By being told we're too young so many times, we actually start to believe it. You've probably been told over and over during your life how you need more experience, more education, and more life skills, before you can reach your goal. However, by the time you have everything "they" say you need, the rules of the game will have changed! In the meantime, during all those years of trying to get more of whatever you are supposed to have, your creativity will have fizzled out as self-doubt takes over. The "more" of everything you are told to have will act as a downer to creativity, initiative, assertiveness, and definitely to the desire to succeed in life and even to succeed in society!

You're young, so what? Stop accepting this as a disadvantage and start using it to your advantage in life!

How do you find the resources to do this? How do you find the drive to continue when you're talked out of it? Believe you're not too young! There are plenty of young people who saw their dreams become reality. They didn't listen to the masses; they didn't stop and think they couldn't succeed with their plan. Obstacles happened, of course, but they climbed over them or went around them. It honestly amazes me how fast someone will give up everything they have worked for the moment there's a bump in the road.

When you learn about your field of interest and even find a way, such as interning or doing errands to get employment in that field, it builds a sense of dependability for others to examine, while giving you a sense of worth for your inner self. It really doesn't matter what the job happens to be—if you're at your chosen business place and you start there as a floor sweeper, it's perfectly okay! The reason it's okay is because your energy will push you up into more responsible roles within the business. While you don't want to be a floor sweeper forever, you do want to work in the business where you got the sweeper job. So, just do your job well and you'll rise within the business.

It's important, however, to not just do your job well, but to also make a positive footprint. Watch everything and everyone. Do errands, even if it's just grabbing coffee for a snarky boss. Make yourself as indispensable as you possibly can. Yes, you may get refusals, and yes, they may say there are age restrictions or there's nothing you can do at the moment, but be there with the offer every time. Make them realize their mistake by showing up early and asking how you can help.

It took me a dozen tries to get a morning show internship at a popular radio station, called the "VYBE," when I was in high school. After I got the internship, I never rolled my eyes at the DJs with diva attitudes. I never refused to do a task demanded of me. I stopped counting the number of times I was belittled or totally ignored by the DJs. By that time, I had interviewed more than 500 celebrities, on location, in all parts of the country, as well as producing shows and dealing with executives from Las Vegas to New York City, all of whom this small radio station and its DJs knew. However, they always seemed to get joy out of playing the game of ignoring my presence or having me do mundane tasks. I found it humiliating, but I never let on or called them out for it. I was happy being at the radio station. Dealing with control issues or head games wasn't something I was happy about, but it wasn't a deal-breaker for me either. When I quit working there, I prophesied they'd still have the same jobs, doing the same tasks, in the same small station ten years later. Although it's only been five years, so far I've been eerily right about that.

Few people find their special talent/passion/gift, or whatever you want to call it, at a really young age. Others search their whole life, wondering and self-doubting whether or not their talent can be leveraged into a successful career. Some conform by morphing their talent into what society wants from them. The main thing to be aware of as Millennials and Gen Zers is that your age *IS* the power. You have what many in society lack—youth, creativity, dreams, and energy!

It's never too soon to start surrounding yourself with people who you are interested in being like, or who are in a field you are interested in pursuing. The saying, "You are the average of your closest friends," is such a real saying! If you surround yourself with unmotivated people, negative people, or people with no serious direction in life, I promise you that shit will rub off on you like glitter! And it will be just as hard to get rid of, too.

I have found it's often better to be alone or limit hangouts with those kinds of people than to be around them. You can learn so much about those around you, and yourself, when you start spending a lot of quality "alone" time. Shedding people who are dead weight may sound cruel, but you need to use part of your alone time planning how to spend your social or extra time with people who are in the same mindset/career path as yourself. Finding people who are in your field of interest is crucial to developing yourself and your future, in my opinion. Time may be on your side, but you must be specific with who you give your time to and how you invest it.

I started my radio show when I was eleven years old and soon learned about all the behind-the-scenes issues. In addition, the people I interviewed taught me a lot and are the reason I'm who I am today. They were a lot older than me, and professionals in their fields, so besides giving me great advice before and after our interviews, they also taught me life skills.

Legendary country music singer Charlie Daniels chatted with me a few times in his touring RV over the years and one thing we talked about was sacrifice. If you choose a career, especially early on, learn to display discipline. I know Millennials older than me who still have mixed up priorities. Their discipline in life and career are non-existent.

Growing up, before I chose radio for a career, I was training to be a professional ballerina. By the age of ten, I was spending more hours in the dance studio than at home or school and, as the years went by, the hours and intensity increased as well. While multitasking with dance and my radio show, I understood discipline. There were multiple times per week that I booked interviews with celebrities and missed countless sleepovers, birthday parties, and family time. I considered myself a quasi-professional with discipline.

Charlie Daniels reminded me to realize there are only so many hours in the day. You're going to have to choose.

Will it be a friend's birthday party or editing video to meet a deadline that you make the priority? You're not going to be able to do it all, and people around you won't understand what you choose to make your obligation. You'll lose friends, which is a tough choice for a pre-teen.

What I was doing on the radio wasn't cool. It was also the most unrelatable career I could have chosen in middle/high school. I was known as the "radio girl" at the time and I absolutely hated it. The average girl my age was going shopping, participating in cheerleading, and talking about boy crushes at slumber parties. Our youth can be used to our advantage, but that doesn't mean every young person will be able to relate. Your tenacity in pursuing your dreams may alienate you from just about everyone around you. So, be prepared to *not* find understanding with peers. Your outlet for conversation will be almost nonexistent in your age range.

Gary Vaynerchuk, an author, motivational speaker, and internet personality, told me in an interview how he spent his twenties with no social life or exciting vacations at all. Instead, it was constant work for him to build his career. Tenacity is great, but there's a personal price you have to be prepared for as well. This is another reason to surround yourself with people you are interested in, as well as people in your field of interest, to see if it really is something you want to pursue. You may find (and probably will find) it's not as glamorous as you thought it would be!

The few people who did think what I was doing was amazing had no idea how hard I worked and how much time it took. These, of course, are some of the negative aspects of dealing with pursuing your talent or passion. It is difficult and the lack of being mainstream will confuse you. But, ultimately, if you come through the early trying times, the success you achieve will be worth it. Most importantly, you'll learn so much along the way that has nothing to do with the knowledge you gain in school and everything to do with bettering yourself with life skills.

Dr. Karl Pillemer, a gerontologist at Cornell University and author of *30 Lessons for Living: Tried and True Advice from the Wisest Americans*, interviewed 1,500 people over the age of sixty-five about what haunts them most concerning their life choices. It all comes down to how they used their time. Pillemer found the number one biggest regret was not spending enough *time* choosing the correct life partner. Second was not resolving a family dispute, thinking there's plenty of *time* to get to that "someday." Third was spending too much *time* worrying.

Making positive use of your youth (translation: *time*), gives you a major edge over your peers. Making good use of your time when you're young can lead to a lot of great things happening, and it can put you way ahead of the game! I'm going to suggest Millennials and Gen Zers will, most likely, look back in fifty years and say they wish they hadn't wasted so much time on social media coveting other peoples' lives, such as the Kardashians!

Singer and songwriter, Ed Sheeran, told me when I was fourteen years old to keep doing what I was doing, and that I'd be at the top by the time my eighteenth birthday came around. He was a year off, but the principle philosophy is use time to your advantage and work hard at your passion, and it'll benefit you in the near future.

Young entrepreneur and the author of *Winning at a Young Age,* Robert Bechsgaard, says there are two things, two habits that have been key to him being successful.

1. Learning:

"First, is learning. Way too many people know about this but don't implement it. I love reading books and learning through videos."[1]

2. Preparation:

"The second thing is plan out my day every night before. This helps me stay focused and motivated all throughout the day."[2]

Achieving a system of productivity gives you an edge over others who are unfocused and unable to "get their shit together." Sometimes simple is the easiest commitment.

Being young in the game isn't something to apologize about. Don't hold back the initiative you are wanting others to recognize in you. You need to be bold and believe in yourself. Surround yourself with others who are like-minded and group yourself with those whom you wish to be like, such as your 'circle of achievers.' They will recognize your drive and help you solidify your success, despite your young age. Millennials and Gen Z's are impatient, but not always as calculated as they should be. Maintain discipline in your youth, aim high, and enjoy the journey!

CHAPTER 2

Refocus from the Negative

We've all had dreams, and we've all had those dreams crushed or threatened to be crushed. And sometimes we've had those dreams crushed by well-meaning family members who don't want us to experience failure. Other times it's by peers or acquaintances who look at what we're doing as crazy. The excitement of our dreams wears off quickly and our end-goal seems miles away. The effort it takes to achieve those dreams seems overwhelming.

All those negative voices come into your head and your own doubting voices play into those voices. They tell you it's too hard, you don't need to do it, and it won't change, or you're going about it all the wrong way. Your journey seems impossible and now you're questioning everything. The desires and purpose you felt before are smashed up, like someone dropped a bowl of Jell-O on the floor. It's just a big sticky mess and you don't know what to do. This is where you have to accept that negative feedback will be a part of life. It's not going to end. So, it's vitally important to look at ourselves and prepare. It isn't easy. Nothing worthwhile is easy.

The first part of navigating the negativity comes by looking at yourself. You have to prepare for the obstacles, as well as the negative vibes you'll get from others who try to shake your will and destroy your true self from the greatness you're hoping to achieve.

You must prepare yourself like a racehorse! Visualize the finish line and let yourself feel the win. Don't think of the other racehorses or the crowd yelling. Those are only distractions to get in your head, trying to force you to drop out of the race.

I made this mistake when I was Student Government President in high school and then re-running for the same position my sophomore year. My opponent was a popular guy who always had the teachers laughing. I went into the election confident I'd beat him—until he discovered a music video I posted when I was nine years old. I had a high-pitched voice and was singing about my chihuahuas. He showed the video around school and told people, in a snarky fashion, "See, she's off doing this kind of stuff and doesn't have time to be president." Other students began singing the video lyrics in the hallways and creeping a look at me with laughter. Of course, it psyched me out mentally and I lost focus. It hurt me emotionally and I lost my mental vision of winning. If I could go back in time, I would tell my fourteen-year-old self to look and act like a racehorse, focusing on the finish line rather than freezing up like a deer caught in the headlights and fearing the oncoming doom.

This is where mentors come into play. A good mentor is like a jockey who can lead you through the thumping herd of horses. A mentor can advise you to take this turn cautiously, or squeeze in between the other racehorses with a burst of energy when the timing is right. They can help with your confusion and declutter your anxiety because they understand your goal. They understand how your effort and energy need to go from focusing on the negative to focusing on the productive and positive.

If you think of all the bad days you've survived, then you'll recognize your survival rate is 100%! Think about that. Everything you thought was going to be the end of you was not the end of you. How can you be so sure? Well, you're reading this book, so that's proof you survived. You survived all the negative influences. You even survived all your own self-doubt. Most people stop when they get negative thoughts, whether of their own doing or planted by other people. This is especially evident with Millennials and Gen Zers.

It's time to go beyond just surviving—we can change the way we think! We have to be that racehorse keeping our eyes on the finish line. We can't buy into the gloom, doom, and negativity people surround us with so much of the time. We have to learn how to dodge the negative before it ever gets a chance to touch us. We have to change the way we think!

So how do you block out negativity? While interviewing Heather Monahan, author of *Creating Confidence*, on my podcast, *If God Had A Podcast*, I learned a simple trick— the power of sticky notes! She told me that in order to build confidence and block out the negativity, I should jot down on a sticky note how thankful I am. Corny huh? But this simple trick is what most professionals swear by.

The best time to do this is before you leave in the morning to start your day. The task fortifies your mind with a layer of good vibes! Think gratitude! Jot down everything you have to be grateful or thankful for in your life. What do you have going for you?

➢ You have your health,
➢ A job,
➢ A supportive family,
➢ You woke up this morning,
➢ You don't have cavities,
➢ Etc., etc.

We all have things we can be grateful for in life. Whatever it is that you are grateful for in your life, jot it down! Find those little, or big, blessings first thing each morning and use your gratitude as fuel to start your day more positive and productive! Be grateful for what you have and the ability you have to achieve more! Your ability to dream is a big thing to be grateful for every day.

> "Imagination is everything—it is the
> preview to life's coming attractions."
> ~ Albert Einstein ~

When we bog ourselves down with negative thoughts, we can go from racehorse to pack mule in an instant. The pack mule doesn't have any dreams to win. The pack mule doesn't imagine itself crossing the finish line. There's not even a finish line on the pack mule's horizon. The only thing it does is accept the load piled on its back until it has become so heavy there's nothing else it can think of at that time.

Don't buy into the negativity! Negativity dampers your imagination, and lack of imagination clouds your vision. Without a vision you cannot have a dream. By throwing off the weight of all those negative feelings, you'll find yourself able to focus on the race at hand. You'll once again get the finish line in your focus and race towards it.

By releasing all those negative feelings, you're able to focus and win your race. You're able to achieve the steps to your dream. You're able to have faith in yourself to achieve your goals.

"Faith is the substance of things hoped for,
the evidence of things not seen."
~ Hebrew 11:1 ~

This kind of faith or patience is difficult for the twenty-somethings. It's hard for them to overcome because Millennials and Gen Zers just want everything fast. The words *patience* and *Millennials* aren't often used in the same sentence. But, we need to have this kind of faith and this kind of patience for imagination to blossom.

Patience, faith, and jotting down the good things in life? Does it all sound too simple to be effective? Sometimes it is the simplest things that can make the largest impacts over time. A small hole in a dam is patched and it maintains the integrity of the dam for years to come. But if that hole is never patched, the water will flow through the crack until it grows larger and larger, eventually destroying the dam and everything it was intended to protect.

All too often, we allow negativity to seep into us, day after day, little by little, until it eventually breaks something inside, destroying all we were hoping and dreaming about. Millennials and Gen Zers have whole new levels of negativity to navigate. Unlike generations before us, our negativity is not limited to a bully in the hallway, a family member who cannot relate to our dreams, or a sibling mocking our awkward attempts to achieve our goals.

Technology has opened a portal for complete strangers across the world to add their negativity in our lives.

Negativity is the crazy horse running next to us in this race. The crazy horse that keeps trying to bite at us until it takes us out. Stop the distractions! Learn how to maintain your peace throughout your day. You've jotted down your "happy thoughts" and now it's time to spread your wings and fly down the course to the finish line!

Once again, utilize the voice of a mentor. Have someone you trust and can confide in with the negative you receive. A good mentor will help you set healthy boundaries to help keep you on track and keep you from getting "bitten" and taken out by negativity. They help you identify the tools you have at your disposal to succeed.

In the beginning of this chapter, I mentioned how negativity won't go away. It is interwoven into the threads of life and is bound to present itself at one time or another. It is not limited to destroying our dreams. We must be aware that when it is given power, it can wipe us out entirely.

I talked with singer Kenny Loggins about some negative issues he had to deal with before. He had a huge overbite (like Freddy Mercury) and the negative effects (from peers and the public) tended to make him self-conscious and a little introverted. Negativity was altering who he was as a person.

We see this happen so much on social media. Someone posts about an event they attended, a vacation they're experiencing, or just their everyday life. They have some people who like what they're doing, but they've also exposed themselves to the negative naysayers who call them out on using a bad filter, one-up their experience, or flat out send them hate.

Overcoming negativity isn't just about achieving dreams and goals. It's about navigating this life standing up, instead of arm-crawling through defeat after defeat. It's so discouraging to see someone barely out of their teens traveling to an exciting place, such as Hawaii, and discrediting or disregarding the experience because someone bummed them out with a comment about a bad filter.

"...people can have a negative influence on the way you think, feel and behave, affecting your emotional balance, because you gave them too much power in your life. And, as their control grows, you dwarf more."[3]

I can totally relate to that!

When someone says, "You look beautiful," I love the compliment and it's a great high for a few minutes. But, when someone says, "Wow, what happened to you? Have you been sick?" I will literally be in a state of gloom for the rest of the day and book a facial, regardless of my schedule! Truly, people can be abrasively weird with their questions, but it happens.

Those negative vibes have a way of propagating around people, too. Someone may comment negatively about you because they are feeling negative. Say you are feeling optimistic about your day and you're at Starbucks with your laptop, going over strategy for your latest project. A friend pops up behind you and, looking over your shoulder at what you're doing, asks, "Hey, what's that?" You calmly explain some of the project's dynamics in layman's terms, trying unsuccessfully to keep the excitement out of your voice.

They frown at it for a minute and say something like, "Well, okay, so why are you doing that instead of blah, blah." Somehow, they manage to squash your enthusiasm with one sentence. Popped the balloon. You just stare at them like, "Wow." Your ideas, goals, and dreams feel shriveled up, like Ursula's collection of clams.

I have found out, all too often, how friends have a way of being *discouraging* more than *encouraging*. It's always harder to shrug off the negativity they plant in you. When we are younger, negativity most often comes from friends and family. As we grow older, we find it more from friends and co-workers since they are the people we are around the most. They are the ones who say both the nicest and worst things to us. Most of the time, they are not intending to plant negativity, but it happens.

What I have found to protect against those negative vibes infiltrating my psyche for any period of time is surprisingly easy: It's called *awareness*. You have to be aware of this natural instinct to soak up the negativity of another. By being aware of the impact, you can shield or protect yourself. Take what they say under consideration and file it in your mental box. I used to be sensitive to feedback, or even general conversations I'd have with people about what I do. It really bothered me. Peripheral feedback was important to me. Negativity made me more vulnerable and hazier about my goals.

After I realized this, I began to avoid people who loaded me down with negative vibes. As for those I could not avoid, I learned to apply a layer of mental sunblock so I didn't get "burned" by their words.

Acknowledging negativity is a part of life that will always exist, and it is the first step in throwing off its weight. Creating a list of things we are grateful or thankful for is the easiest way to set our sights on the finish line for our goals and dreams. But, most importantly, it's what makes us "us."

Accepting that the people closest to us will most likely be the ones to intentionally, or unintentionally, spray us with the negative fairy dust of gloom helps us prepare for what's coming.

Negativity can kill our dreams and creativity in one deathly swoop. It threatens our hopes and way of life. It's contagious and you never want, or need, to breathe that virus in!

We must, as my nutritionist Lorraine says, "Protect our energy." She says, "You are the most important person to defend, so don't let negativity get to you, babe. You got great stuff to do!"

And, the same is true for you!

CHAPTER 3

You've Got a Dream? Awesome – Now Make It Happen!

Every successful person that I've talked to, and definitely every famous person I have talked to, all had one thing in common. This thing they had in common is that it didn't matter if they came from a poor background or a rich one. It didn't matter if they had college degrees or happened to be high school dropouts. It didn't matter if they came from a dysfunctional family life or a supportive and loving family. What successful and famous people had in common was *commitment* to their craft /passion/ gift. It required their total commitment, whether they happened to be a singer, author, pro sports figure, or entrepreneur.

You have to commit to yourself and, as I mentioned in the last chapter, this will require blocking out the negative voices. It requires being able to ride the storms, deal with the dynamics, and continue to believe in yourself and what you are doing. The commitment requires taking a leap when you need to do so and having faith in yourself to reach for the next level or new chapter. Sometimes you're able to seek advice from others who can help, but sometimes there's part of this journey you end up doing solo.

I interviewed Steve Forbes, Chief Executive of Forbes Media LLC, when I was fourteen years old. When he told me that in order to be successful you need to take risks, I was shocked. Forbes was probably the most conservative person I'd ever interviewed. He was all business, professional and serious. I went into the interview afraid I would mess something up. This was a stark contrast to my earlier, more laid-back interviews with people in the music industry, such as Ziggy Marley, Sublime, or Kevin Jonas. Forbes calmly said, "Don't be afraid to take those risks." I mulled over his advice and some of the other tips he gave me over the next few days. I think that's when I made the permanent commitment to pursue media instead of continuing with a professional dance career.

After dedicating seven years of my life to dance, with a concentration in ballet, I reached a crossroads. I could continue with dance, which would require adding more hours by having online school/homeschool offered at the dance studio. Or, I could remain in public school and start the International Baccalaureate program I was accepted into at the time.

This was my crossroads. It wasn't about choosing between something you like a lot and something you don't like at all. Instead, it was choosing between two things I very much enjoyed. Those are some of the most difficult crossroads we encounter. At the moment of this particular crossroad, dance had defined me. "Pavlina Ballerina" is who I was at that time. It would have been so easy to continue with dance and let go of my media career. Even with all the interviews I had conducted, media didn't seem like the logical route because I had already dedicated so much of my time to ballet. Letting go of ballet would require me to completely redefine myself.

I decided to let go of dance. At the time, it felt a little alien and kind of clunky. Was I making the right decision or screwing up my life? The thought of change and the unknown was scary, plus no one around me understood my decision. But it turned out to be the right decision. Two years later, I began interning for Sean Hannity. The following year, I got an internship with iHeart Radio in New York City. And a couple months after that, I was offered a permanent position at another major media network, The Salem Media Group.

There were times over the years when it challenged me. That's when I had to fall onto the commitment I had made to myself. I had committed to pursue a career in media. No takebacks. I had to keep going!

Reaching your own commitment requires preparing yourself for the good and bad days. It's a simple thing we are told, but oftentimes forget to prepare for it. There

WILL be good days and there WILL be bad days. So simple, and yet I've seen so many friends who hit one blip on their timeline and find themselves spiraling out of control. They had goals that were reachable and very possible to obtain, but then a bad day sucker punches them and they get discouraged and depressed, go into debt, become unmotivated, and lose the spark of creativity that made them so unique. It's the same spark that had helped them believe they could reach their initial goals.

So, if we know life will throw us some sucker punches here and there, how do we achieve the commitments we make to ourselves? As for me, it was to sit down and come up with a plan. My plan included small, synchronized goals that were both short term and long term. And, of course, a technicolor big picture.

At *The House of Blues* in Lake Buena Vista, there was a new band performing called *Imagine Dragons*. It was 2012 and this was their first national tour. No one had really heard of them, but they were playing at some small/medium venues before their album hit. Before their performance, I talked to lead singer Dan Reynolds. He's a tall, soft-spoken performer, and humble.

> *Pavlina:* If you could put a vision or dream board on your tour bus, what would you put on it, for *Imagine Dragons,* that you would want to accomplish?

Dan Reynolds: Those are good questions. Yeah, you know, we'd probably put a picture of the world. I think we want to see the world and start to play around the world more (from *IMAGINE DRAGONS'* Dan Reynolds Interview w/Pavlina, House of Blues, Orlando 2012).

Well, I think it's safe to say, that vision board did him some good, because the band certainly reached worldwide fame.

Things don't just happen (okay, maybe sometimes they do just happen), and especially with a few of the social media stars I've talked with in the past. But as a rule, there's a commitment you have to establish for yourself, to help keep you on track with where you want to go. On top of that, you must have grit that helps keep you focused on your endeavor so that no matter what, I repeat, NO MATTER WHAT—despite the obstacles, getting thrown under the bus by colleagues, the unexpected dynamics, etc.—you carry on.

I mentioned the commitment to yourself, but you're probably wondering what is necessary with commitment to others. You need to be a team player, because it works out best for you in the end. The people around you need to see your commitment. You may forget you're young, but others won't! Older people—your parents, your boss, your professors at school—watch your actions a lot more than you think they do! I remember being told, the minute you step out to the venue, you're on and need to be professional, which is a reminder that people are already starting to form their opinions of you. I was watched for how I approached security, and how I negotiated and dealt with the personnel backstage at concerts, as well as my handling of VIP areas at conference centers.

The commitment you have to yourself to continually do the job is definitely important, but that needs to extend to the people around you and those you interact with as well. Author and Former NBC Nightly News Anchor Tom Brokaw said to me after our interview, "You know, I wasn't going to do the interview with you. I don't like doing interviews, but I watched how you handled the crowd to get to me. My decision was made."

Having people around me who prejudging me irked me at first. It also made me sensitive about judging others. After conducting a few hundred celebrity interviews, I knew how to read people fairly well. And for many, it was a matter of proving myself to be professional and knowledgeable enough to do the job. It's not that people don't trust you, they just have their own timeframe and seal of approval indicating acceptance. Some people are quick with their acceptance, but others will put you through obstacle courses and throw you under the bus a few times when the boss isn't looking. Not going to take it?

Okay, then walk. It's definitely easier not to take it! But, commitment is part of the journey and, no, it's not always easy or fair.

I call commitment your belief in your grit recipe. It's also something you may find needs to be a little elastic. Most Millennials (67%) and Generation Zers (40%) feel pressured to succeed.[4] So, any added requirements can frustrate the average twenty-something person. But, the best way to add this commitment to yourself and others, into your regimen or regular lifestyle, is to start daily with it. Establish your commitment and have it be like a mission statement, and put it where you can see it every day. Your commitment to others is less visual. Try to establish a more professional attitude and appearance if needed, and step up to the challenge before you.

The other thing important in commitment is to outline your set of goals. Dr. Marilyn Price-Mitchell wrote in *Psychology Today* about the importance of goal setting. It's the road map to success. Research has shown that setting goals is linked to self-confidence, motivation, and independent decision-making.

Psychologist Gail Matthews did a study in 2015 that showed how people who wrote down their goals were 33% more likely to achieve them than people who only formulated them in their heads. A few steps with goal setting is fairly easy to accomplish.

First, write your goals down. Writing your goals down is more concrete, and then when you achieve each goal, it gives you more of a sense of satisfaction and self-worth, as well as a more solid commitment. There are even apps to help make it easy and do it with the convenience of your phone.

Second, goals should be specific, but reachable. They shouldn't be "pie in the sky" type goals because that detracts from the commitment and can be discouraging. Challenge yourself, but don't reach for lofty ideals.

Finally, look at and reexamine your goals often and discuss them with a mentor. It's okay for them to be elastic.

When I decided to take on the *Guinness Book of World Records* for "most radio interview in 24 hours," I had a specific goal I wanted to achieve. I managed to break the record, with 347 interviews within the timeframe, but there was a lot of preparation ahead of time. It was preparation where I graphed out the "what if" moments. Since the event was conducted outside and had to be continuous, I looked at the possibility of a power failure or equipment failure. There was also a possibility of man power negligence. I analyzed everything I could control, and planned for backup resources. I considered everything for which I was directly responsible because only I could make, or break, the record. This included basic things such as how to stay awake and diligently pursue what was required during the twenty-four-hour time period. I had to think about how much I'd need to do to break the record and how much would be needed to blow the record out of the ballpark. Once I broke the record, it such a strong adrenaline rush in me that I probably could have continued for another twenty-four hours! Once my goal was met, I had a renewed energy and focus to do more goal-setting.

Olympic swimming champion Michael Phelps talked about setting goals as being important for himself, not for others.

> "It's about what I want to do, it's not about what someone else wants me to do. And, if I come up short, then I'm just going to readjust my goals and hopefully get there sometime in the future."
> ~ Michael Phelps ~

Goals are crucial to the commitment you make, but the goals don't have to be to become the next superstar. I interviewed the iconic Grammy Hall of Fame singing group, *The O'Jays* ("Love Train," "For the Love of Money"), backstage before one of their concerts. Their goal was simply to be able to eat and get some shoes! That's why they started singing and performing! They definitely reached their goals, as well as achieving Gold and Platinum songs of the 1970s.

When I was about twelve years old, I drew a picture of a house with flowers in the garden, and a few sprigs of grass. There were paned windows I drew on the house and a chimney on top, with smoke coming out in little puffs. In the sky, there were puffy clouds, birds flying, and a big yellow sun. I asked my mom where I was with my career.

By then, my radio show was growing and I side-hustled as a steel drum street performer, with quite a few gigs every week. I was still in the dance studio about twenty hours a week as well. I look back and wonder how I had time to breathe, but I loved the constant, busy pace of doing so many things.

But, back to my picture of the house. My mom understood my question from the drawing, because she pointed to the flowers and said, "You're right here, but someday you're going to be that bird in the sky." This was a drawing I referred to over and over in the years that followed. The commitment you make will grow into a higher success, as you continue your journey. It will also create a level of protection when you have your failures, because you'll be able to handle those setbacks and come back even stronger!

As Les Brown says, "You gotta be hungry!" If you lack commitment, drive, or inner grit, then you won't have the strength to persevere through all the tough times, the negativities, the self-doubt, and the odd roller coaster of your journey. It's the commitment, in my opinion, that is the framework to your house of success.

CHAPTER 4

Face It, You're Gonna Fail

At Steve Harvey's Disney event, where I was one of the *2014 Disney Dreamers Academy*, the theme of the guest speakers, as well as Harvey, was to *Fall Hard/Fall Fast*. At the time, I found this theme confusing and a little discouraging. Why would I want to *Fall Hard/Fall Fast*? What if I couldn't pull myself back up again? What if the media had shifted and I wasn't accepted for my originality by the time I recovered? No one wants to fail, do they?

As much as I wanted to believe everyone was okay with failure, I couldn't face mine, which is why I got stuck on this chapter when writing this book. So, a week went by, then a few more weeks, and then a month. I didn't even want to do this book anymore because I couldn't get started with this chapter. I was done with it and didn't want to write about anything or talk about it. And then it came to me—I'm my own worst enemy and my biggest obstacle!

Teenagers and twenty-somethings have the same thing in common now that wasn't so present with previous generations—impatience, entitlement, and a lack of confidence. Yeah, I know, that's a bag of mixed up shit but that's why we're messed up. Entitlement is such an over-used word now, but it's the biggest truth. We weren't born feeling entitled. No, we were spoon-fed this monstrosity all through our school lives. We got a medal for finishing last, for God's sake! Why? We lost but were still told we were wonderful. We got participation trophies just because we showed up!

Then, real life comes at us and the boss doesn't give us anything for "just showing up." Even if we take a menial job that feels like our next assignment is to mop the floor with our tongues we figure, "Okay, so when's my promotion. I deserve more." We find ourselves loaded down and drowning in self-doubt because we have known nothing except the smoke and mirrors of false success.

I remember talking to Barbara Corcoran, best known for TV's *Shark Tank*, and she emphatically stated she'd much rather employ or invest in someone who has failed and rose up from that failure, than have a Harvard graduate. There's not a lot of us that fall into that category because most of us are so afraid we'll fail, we never even try.

Social media further adds to the smoke and mirrors that has become our reality. Our focus and energy is to make ourselves a template of a fake person, with a fake life, and we judge each other by that fake person created on social media. That's why we fail and can't get up. That's why there's a suicide every forty-five seconds. That's why I'm on a rant about failing that covers way too much, except to say you need to face your worst enemy and realize it's not all your fault. But, you also need to pull yourself up and deal with it. Don't crumble from it. Learn from it and get stronger.

I didn't have any absolutely big failures. I wasn't homeless or lost a ton of money or flunked out of school. What I did have was a lot of toxic people and negativity around me. This gave me (at the least little road blocks) a lot of self-doubt. Should I be doing something else? Do people know something I don't, like I'm really bad at my career, or what?

I wasn't sensitive at a young age. So, when a pair of dance teachers said I wasn't any good, I just worked that much harder. Bloody feet from hours of dancing grossed out my mom, but to me it was just a sign of working hard and getting better. At age eleven, I began street performing and started my radio show. The dance moms and other kids were so incredibly mean because I was doing something different. In their opinions, it was all about dance and nothing else. Everything else was insignificant because it was a tight bubble of dance culture. Honestly, it was suffocating because it was so one dimensional. But, I kept doing it all—public school, dance for fifteen-to-twenty hours a week, a radio show, and on-location interviews with celebrities—every week. By this time, I had dropped karate after I got the black belt, and stopped gymnastics when it got to a higher level requiring more time. People were concerned I might burn out, but I honestly liked the variety and high intensity of everything. It taught me time management, leadership skills, handling quick decisions, and talking to every type of person about everything.

My biggest failure was when I let myself believe I might not be good at media. People were spreading stupid rumors that my dad was rich and paying people so I could get my interviews. Other people said I got my interviews because my mom worked for Lady Gaga. All of this was totally absurd and untrue, but that didn't make it any easier to hear.

Of course, the people within the dance world were the worst. I don't think they really intended any harm, but for those people dance was their life, so they had no understanding of why I'd choose to "throw away" an opportunity in ballet for something foreign such as a radio career. Their questions only solidified my own insecurities regarding my choice. Was I even good at radio interviews? I didn't know. I had nobody to train me.

Ballet had a distinct discipline that wasn't present in media. You learn the moves, you practice the moves, you rinse and repeat over and over and over again. Radio interviews changed from person to person. No two interviews were exactly alike. I had no manual. I had no "moves" handed down from instructor to student to repeat over and over again throughout the years. I was self-taught, and that made the self-doubt all the more crippling.

Thankfully, I had my mom standing in my corner and supporting me through it all. She had no idea what I was doing or how to help me navigate through my career choice, but she did an amazing job of encouraging me every step of the way. Unfortunately, I made a decision to move away from that daily support. It was needed, as we all have to spread our wings and leave the nest someday. My decision took me from the small suburbs of Florida to the big-city madness of New York.

I had just turned eighteen years old and it was no longer ballerinas and dance moms giving me grief about my decision. In fact, during my time in college, nobody was saying anything about my career choice. But, I found myself even worse off. I was surrounded by new friends who were plagued with depression and anxiety. Nothing they did was ever going to be good enough in their eyes. They were constantly focused on the negative, which made me think I should be as well. I began questioning my career direction (again), my academic direction, and my personal worth. It robbed me of my energy to go on.

This melted into a state of darkness no one else even knew about. No one was discouraging me. My own self-doubt was feeding off every negative comment I observed from others around me. If they were doubting their choices, I should be too. If they were anxious and depressed, that was probably the norm for someone my age. My ears honed in on everything negative and played it over and over again while discounting anything positive as unworthy to hold on to at that time. So, for real, it was a dark period. So, how do you get out of a failure?

Pavlina: What's one word you would use to describe a successful entrepreneur?

Barbara Corcoran: Insecurity. I would say give me a person who's insecure, has something to prove, hates the bosses they work for, doesn't really want to have what was given to them in life, and they're afraid to death to try something. Give me that guy—push him off a cliff—and watch what he does. People are always much stronger than they give themselves credit for (from BARBARA CORCORAN Interview at ASI, Orlando 2014 with Pavlina).

Regardless of the failure, you have to believe in yourself. You're stronger and smarter than you think. Really! One year can make a difference. One month can make a difference. Even one day can change things you never thought would happen!

Write down different ways to cope with your failure. Consider meditation—putting the failure into perspective and seeing something positive from the failure. Then, visualize yourself achieving your goal and this failure will only be an obstacle you can overcome.

We all have setbacks and negative events we label as failures. It can be a personal or professional setback, but Psychologist Martin Seligman found there are "three Ps" that can stunt our recovery:

1. Personalization – The belief that we are at fault.

2. Pervasiveness – The belief that an event will affect all areas of our lives.

3. Permanent – The belief that the aftershocks will last forever.

By accepting these three Ps, we cripple ourselves from the failure. We're damaged, not just from the setback or failure—we have also killed any future because we play, and replay, the three Ps in our heads, over and over again. You say to yourself, "It's my fault that my life is awful, and it's going to continue being awful." You have to recognize that the setback wasn't entirely your fault and it shouldn't have the power to impact your future. It's not personal, it's not pervasive, and it's not permanent! You can, and will, overcome it!

Now, I know you're probably thinking, "But seriously, Pavlina, what if I can't overcome the failure? Then what?" That's what I would have been thinking a few years back.

Remember that "dark" period I talked about earlier? Well, when I say dark, it was completely void of hope for me. I was even suicidal at the time because things seemed so hopeless. It was during this time that I called home and had a conversation with my dad. My dad was, and still is, a man of few words. So, when I called to inform him I should probably talk to a therapist because I wasn't sure what to do, he dug into his Lebanese roots and dished out an old Arabic saying.

The saying talks of someone going into the water to drown himself/herself. But, once in the water, that same person begins fighting back because they actually want to live. My takeaway from the saying is that subconsciously there is a part of yourself you don't like and you want to kill off. But the moment you get into the water, you realize how that small piece doesn't equal *all* of who you are as a person. When this revelation takes place, you decide to fight for the rest of you. Setbacks, negative events, and failures do not make up the whole of who you are as an individual. You can, and will, overcome any failures, but only if you choose to fight!

"You do not drown by falling in the water;
you drown by staying there."
~ Edwin Louis Cole ~

There was an interview I thought was a total failure. It wasn't a bad interview, but the events leading up to it seemed ... off to me. So, in my mind it was a failure. It had been an average day in middle school, followed by dance at the ballet school. The interview was at *Epcot*, one of Disney's theme parks in Orlando. It was a hot day, like most days are in Florida. I hadn't eaten since lunch at school and I was beyond tired. I met up with Disney security, who escorted me over to the property area. It was an outside concert, in the back of the park. The heat and fatigue got to me and after security left, I promptly bent over in the immaculate Disney flower beds and threw up. I straightened up, wiped my face, walked over to the backstage area, and said I was ready to do the interview with the singer.

I don't remember anything of that interview, and was actually afraid of passing out. So, I was on autopilot! I felt like a complete failure at doing a worthy job with someone who took the time from their schedule to do this interview. Later, I'd ponder that time and realize I was tougher on myself than I probably should have been. It came mainly from the ballet dancer in me who wanted to achieve perfection and overlook any pain in the process. Ultimately, the takeaway from this isn't to throw up and carry on, but to put one foot in front of the other because you *are* strong, and your strength of character is what should define you, not fear of failure or fear you didn't do well at a particular endeavor. Instead, just keep going.

CHAPTER 5

Stop Searching for Answers and Start Moving

It's so easy to get stuck in your head and get your thoughts all tangled up like a big ball of yarn. Boomers, bless them, are basically uncomplicated people. Things are basically black and white for them. But the Millennials and Gen Zers have been bombarded with information for as long as they can remember. We overcomplicate, overthink, over-stress everything, and it's so easy to do. We feel pulled in different directions, with what our parents expect and with what our peers think is normal. But the biggest elephant in our brain room is what society expects of us! Social media has made us depend on the acceptance and admiration of faceless people. Even eating food has to halt, before we lift up our silverware. We don't pause for a blessing, but rather for a social media posting!

When I was thirteen years old, I was at a venue to interview NBA superstar Shaquille O'Neal. It was, quite honestly, an out-of-control, media-frenzied event that saw me pushed and shoved around like I was a basketball during practice for the Harlem Globetrotters. After a brief interview, amongst the press pool, I caught his publicist and asked if there was any chance I could get a more one-on-one conversation.

Shaquille came over to do our interview and when we finished he said, "You need to make more money on this." After that statement, he sauntered back to meet up with his management, bypassed the frenzied media group, and was gone. The following year, I had the privilege of interviewing his mother, Lucille. They are a family of calm demeanor and great manners. One of the biggest things I took away from the interviews with the O'Neal family is their ability to look at a situation and sum it up in a simple manner.

I had that ability when I was younger. Most kids don't struggle too much with simplicity. As I grew older, though, I lost a lot of my ability for simple analysis and began to overcomplicate and overthink everything. It didn't remain exclusively with career decisions but bled into friendships and academics as well. It got confusing because what was simple reasoning when I was a pre-teen and teen became more complicated. And that just makes no sense! For nearly any quandary in life, we can find an instant answer by googling it. Any query you are stumped on, just google it. So why, in the age of having instant access to high-quality information to help us make decisions, are we still struggling with decision-making?

At a glance, the quick queries we search online immediately suck us into a black hole of link options that can absorb us for hours of hypnotizing research choices. It's like stepping into Ikea for a lightbulb! Of course, there's a label for this perplexing oddity of overload. Psychologist Barry Schwartz labeled it the "Paradox of Choice," an increased level of choice allowing us to achieve objectively better results.

At the same time, however, it also leads to greater anxiety, indecision, paralysis, and dissatisfaction. I would feel overwhelmed from a plethora of information, and that's perfectly normal! The overabundance of information often doesn't empower us to make a more rational choice. Instead, the endless array of options leads us to a greater fear of making the wrong decision. This fear turns on us like an out-of-control snowball going downhill and freezes our analysis into paralysis, thus getting us nowhere fast on decision-making projects. Simply put, you overthink it too much because of the vast amount of information to which you expose yourself and try to absorb. And so you freeze, like a deer caught in headlights.

If you've ever experienced this downside of choice—this paradox of choice leading to chronic indecision—you're not likely to forget the feeling. Neuroscientists have found that analysis paralysis can cripple not just your productivity, but also your mental wellbeing! Our working memory (the focusing we do on information in the moment we're focused on it) is scrapped. It's zapped clean out of our brain. Anxiety and pressure caused by the overwhelming information puts our production on the job, along with self-doubt of failure, spiraling you on the quick ship lollipop of unemployment. Most studies have concluded that Millennials are the biggest generation to suffer anxiety, as we're dubbed the "Therapy Generation." Self-doubt is second nature to many because of the wrapped cocoon quality of life we had growing up, only to later face the real world. But wait, it gets even worse! Besides being young, our asset in the workforce is our creativity. Guess what gets zapped out of us because of the overthinking monster? *Creativity.* Finally, after experiencing the anxiety, self-doubt, and working memory from overthinking—plus having our creativity hit shits creek—we are now exhausted. Decision fatigue spikes and our willpower is depleted. Then, being exhausted, you leave work and experience unhappiness.

So much confusion and exhaustion over decisions—it's crazy. But Millennials and Gen Zers struggle over this to a much greater degree than any other generation. So, what's the best way to handle it?

Prioritize the most important things when you're at your sharpest mentally. Turning decisions that are basic into habits cuts down on thinking about them, which conserves your willpower. Limit the amount of information you are exposed to at any given time. Singer Jessica Simpson lost more than 100 pounds in a few months and everyone was like, "Wow! How'd she do it?" One of the key components to this weight loss was eliminating stress. Simpson's personal trainer, Harley Pasternak, instructed her to turn off her cell phone for an hour each and every day. It's a simple stress reliever my nutritionist also asked me to follow. Before any diet or lifestyle change could take place in the mind and body, the stress had to be controlled.

Analysis paralysis can also be controlled by staying true to yourself.

> Know what makes you unique and stay focused on your goals.
> Understand what's important to you personally and professionally.
> Even go so far as to have your own mission statement for yourself. And, if you need to decide something, refer back to your mission statement to see if the decision aligns with your goals and values.

It's like the vision/board of *Imagine Dragons* lead singer Dan Reynolds. Don't overthink what you want. De-stress yourself, limit your exposure, and prioritize your important decisions or projects. Building habits of some decisions can simplify the clutter as well.

CHAPTER 6

You'll Never Be Happier Than When You Learn to Love Yourself

Love is a mystery to most people. A simple feeling that's the most difficult to achieve, and even harder to hold on to. Millennials know this. They also know they have a difficult battle in loving themselves. In many instances, it's because of society attempting to define them before they've had an opportunity to define themselves. Society wants to attach labels that really don't define Millennials and Gen Zers. Love, like happiness, is just an illusion because their lives are built on social media platforms. We know it's fake, but that doesn't stop continuing the addiction like a bad drug. But wait! How does this relate to self-love?

What's so amazing is how we go about getting self-love. Most of us find it in the simplest form—through social media! It's like a drug addiction, according to Dr. Sara Garofalo. It's a form of escape. Millennials and Generation Zers have to deal with a completely different world than twenty or thirty years ago. The environment now has platforms like Facebook and Instagram that act like hooks. These platforms induce you into a habitual way of behavior. We actually get a "high" from social media.

When we get a pleasant experience from "likes" our brain says "Yeah, let's repeat this!" We're human beings, as well as social animals, so the social "rewards" are activated. This brain activation gives us self-love, but it's a love that's not real. We know it, but we don't want to stop it!

Simon Sinek best describes the process. This digital addiction has our esteem held hostage for another "photo like." Our brain produces dopamine—the "feel good" chemical in our brains. We get a "like" on Facebook, or a comment on our Instagram post, and an instant hit of dopamine rushes through our brain. Our self-esteem, as well as the love we have of ourselves, becomes trapped, waiting for the next hit. Why does this appeal and trap Millennials and Generation Zers more than any other generation? Because first, it's our normal way of life. We've grown up on it and we are dependent on social media. We virtually have no ability or desire to escape it. Second, we are in the age of instant gratification. We want things now and we usually get them. When we don't, we crash. Not only do we crash, but we don't understand the crash and how to come out of the black hole we find ourselves in at the time. Our lives feed on instant everything. Instant shopping at Amazon. Instant dating with Tinder. Instant food via Seamless. We have no patience built into our makeup any more.

How do we re-evaluate ourselves and experience self-love?

We do this by recognizing that "instant" was never intended to be the norm. Experiencing self-love is a slow and steady process to understanding ourselves. It's a process of looking at who we are and appreciating our self-worth. It takes an ability that's alien to us—patience. Take a moment and experience this for yourself. Instead of posting a photo and waiting for a "like," why don't you take a seat and close your eyes. Listen to yourself breathe and become one with yourself. Who are you?

I have found yoga and meditation to be lifesavers in finding self-love. These exercises allow me to experience a stronger sense of peace and build stronger self-esteem. They require me to connect with myself and who I really am, rather than throwing out an image of who I think I am.

Self-love is the foundation of everything we are and everything we have to offer others. In other words, the old adage that says we can't love others until we love ourselves is the framework we build upon in order to have a vital and successful life with ourselves and with others. Social media is a nasty buzzkill because it has the ability to kill our self-worth and acceptance of ourselves.

What makes us special is hidden under a bush because we try so hard to re-make ourselves into what is popular. It's all about what filter makes us look better and more acceptable. Our shortcomings are shriveled and we create a monster of being accepted. We aren't happy with ourselves and we figure no one else would be happy knowing or seeing the "real me." We say to ourselves, "If only I was thinner, richer, prettier, more handsome, stronger," or whatever we covet.

Being happy with ourselves and loving ourselves is a lifelong struggle for Millennials and Generation Zers, because we don't see ourselves as "special." We overlook our uniqueness in society, but it's so crucial to our success in self-love. We spend more time scrolling through other people's lives who we feel are special, all the while discounting our own specialness. Getting lots of social media traction and popular likes isn't self-love, it's a spiraling form of narcissism. Self-aggrandizement creates a fragile framework in our lives and leads to anxiety, depression, and self-hate. It's like we wake up and need a magic potion from the tech witch in order to feel whole and beautiful again.

This is where one has to find a higher power. There is something uplifting and releasing to know your footprint in life is okay, and that you're okay—to realize a higher power accepts your flaws and shortcomings—and to understand there's no pecking order ranking some better than others. There are those who show more commitment to their goals and there are those who show less commitment to their goals, but we are all deserving as human beings. No one is above or below others.

This falls back, in a way, to how Millennials and Generation Zers were brought up. "Everyone's a winner," so we're all great. "Everyone's a winner," however, sets us up for failure when we face a bad day. I mentioned this in an earlier chapter. But, I don't think that was the initial intent. The initial intent was to ensure that no one is left behind. It was to say, "You showed up and gave it your best shot. That is what makes you a winner."

Social media took "Everyone's a winner" and tainted it with a narcissistic filter. Oftentimes, people find themselves trying to "one-up" or "keep up" with others who are posting, rather than trying to be the best they can be. We need to dial it back a little and not take it, or make it, personal. Social media was created as a platform to connect with others, not compete with them. We need to regroup with the social media outlook we create of ourselves and others.

> "Loving yourself and self-love is two
> ways of expressing the nature of God,
> given to every Child of God."
> ~ Pastor Andre Keeley ~

In the need to have self-love comes a need for happiness. It's sort of intertwined in the Millennial and Gen Zer mind. The first place I thought of happiness was in just letting go with laughter. Yeah, I know, we're serious about finding ourselves—spiritual oneness and self-love—and

I take a sharp turn with laughter. But laughter just sort of gets everything back into perspective for us.

I remember when I was to do a phone interview with Shirley Jones. You might recall her from *Hannah Montana* and *The Partridge Family* (David Cassidy's mom on the show, and famous step-mom in real life). She also did a lot of movies and Broadway shows early in her career.

Well, at the time of our interview, her husband, comedian Marty Ingels, was handling the interview for me. Unbeknownst to me, he loved practical jokes. I imagine this serious teen reporter must have seemed like an easy target for his joke. He probably never even stopped to consider how I might be traumatized for life with his simple pursuit of a laugh. Here's how the interview played out:

I make the call. Marty answers. I say who I am and he hangs up. I'm a little confused, maybe something happened to the line, so I call again. He hangs up, again. Finally, on the third try, he hands the phone to Shirley and she explains how her husband is a practical jokester and thought it would be funny to mess with me.

I did my best to shrug it off and continue on with my interview. It was going along fine, until I asked Shirley to tell me a little about herself and being a vegetarian. But, to my surprise, Shirley told me she wasn't a vegetarian. This threw me off and I stumbled through the remainder of the interview. It was obvious that Marty, who I'd vetted all the questions through before the interview, was still working his practical jokes.

I hung up the phone, shaking with embarrassment, but sort of smiling later at how Marty Ingels took both me and Shirley Jones on a comical interview. A few days later, I got a paperback biography of Shirley Jones, autographed personally to me. My mom sent an email thanking Marty for the book. That same day, Marty sent back an email, "Leigh, question: Did we discuss a donation to Shirley's favorite charity or not?"

My mom told me later she sent a donation but was laughing about what a character Marty Ingels happens to be. Sadly, Marty Ingels died three years later. I had to think, when I heard of his passing, that anyone who knew him would definitely be forced into laughter and happiness. He made you think beyond your problems and he did it in such a sweet way. I mention the late Marty Ingels (which most Millennials and Gen Zers won't have any idea about, unless they watch Turner Classic Movies) because he was uncomplicated with the rental space in his head. He just didn't have anyone renting negative space in his brain, unlike so many of us.

Every personal growth expert and life coach will explain how you can't accomplish much, and you certainly can't have self-love, if you always let others influence your behavior or how you see yourself. Your decisions will be influenced by these trashy renters and you'll end up messing up your life with wrong decisions. You can be prone to serious negative thoughts as well, like those I mentioned in Chapter 2. These negative thoughts, and the negative people who get into our heads, can be our worst enemies and stagnate our progress.

To achieve self-love, they can't exist. That is why self-love and spiritual love are combined in this chapter. In my opinion, they work off each other, like yin and yang. Your spiritual love can strengthen your self-love and vice versa. By releasing the negative thoughts and bad renters in our brain, we can move forward, we can achieve our goals, and we can look toward the future. Yes, it's difficult, and yes, we will always have some little voices that are negative, or criticism from someone who is renting space in our head. But, for the most part, there are tools we can implement and habits we can form to help us obtain self-love and spiritual love. We can free our brain space and move forward to produce a positive future in our quality of life and our career.

Why is it so hard to love yourself and be happy? We constantly compare ourselves to others, whether it's their professional success or their body image, in life and on social media. The standards are impossible to follow and keep up with, let alone obtain, in today's world. Believe in something higher, whether it's Buddha, God, the Universe, or the Dalai Lama. I don't care what you believe in at all, just as long as you have some sort of higher power. It will ground you.

Be nice to yourself, because so much of what we say to ourselves affects what we do in our careers and daily lives. We strive for perfection and we say things to ourselves we would never say to other people. Those words control us and can really ruin our day. I challenge you to vocalize it the next time you catch yourself saying something harsh or hurtful to yourself. Know when "enough is enough" because if you simply say, "I will be happy if/when this happens," you will never be happy. The journey is the most enjoyable part, not the end destination.

CHAPTER 7

Think You Can't, and You Won't. Think You Can, and You Will!

Your mindset is another crucial part of the package. I've never seen anyone with only one piece of greatness succeed. Talent is great, but it's not the entire package. Determination and drive are great, but both are really lost without creativity. Creativity is crucial, but it doesn't pave the way to your goal without grit. And the success you work on will be nothing in the end without the ability to love yourself.

It's ultimately like you're juggling, and all the balls need to be in the air, moving in a fluid rhythm. Your mind is programmed to watch them and, after a while, it's second nature. If one of the balls drops, you continue with the rest and pick up the dropped ball when you can add it back to the fold. Jugglers make it look easy, but it's not. Successful people make it look easy, but it's not. So, how do we get this mindset? Do we want it concrete or do we want it elastic?

I mentioned earlier how I participated in the *Disney Dreamers Academy* hosted by Steve Harvey. A group of *100 Disney Dreamers* were chosen out of 10,0000 applicants for this trip to Disney World in Orlando. We were flown to Orlando and given a great time. It was a week of being with Steve Harvey and other influential newsmakers in media and sports who could help us with our career decisions.

One of the crucial speeches Steve Harvey made was about finding your gift. It's totally different than finding your passion! You may totally be passionate about being the next Taylor Swift but sing like a crow. Your gift is what you are good at, without even thinking about it. It's your natural, eyes-closed, you-can-do-better-than-anyone talent. Mine was talking to people. It naturally happened and migrated from good interviews to great ones.

People might see one of my interviews go well for me and not realize there were a whole lot of things that had already transpired before it even began. One of the biggest things is how I had to prove myself for each and every interview. My mindset had to be on point. Every single time. That's what Millennials and Gen Zers really do not comprehend. Your mindset doesn't go on vacation, not even after you achieve your goal or reach the level you are comfortable with for your age. It's a matter of making opportunities happen. It's just a crack in the door to put your foot into, and then continuing onward to find the next opportunity. While maintaining this career climb, we should also enjoy it. I interviewed *Good Morning America* host, and now the host of her new self-titled show, Tamron Hall. The number one piece of advice for a young person she gave me was to "Enjoy the journey."

I started playing steel drums when I was ten years old and quickly had a solid career as a street performer in Daytona Beach, Florida and surrounding areas. One weekend, I was scheduled to perform in New Smyrna Beach. It's a quiet, bohemian-like town, very artsy and famous for surfing. They had a farmer's market every Saturday by the Halifax River. The radio station was always there, under a canopy, and they asked me to perform for an hour or two.

They had other performers in different time slots. I had just arrived and a woman was breaking down her stand and mic. She asked me, "You getting paid for this? I didn't and it's not worth it." I just stared at her. I couldn't understand *not* doing the gig. I loved playing for people, so why not? Even though I didn't get paid, my tips were good, plus the exposure. But, looking at this unhappy performer, I had hugely important rule ingrained in my psyche that would reappear and be echoed by every successful person I've ever met: "You've got to love what you do."

As Oprah Winfrey has been quoted as saying, "If you do work that you love, and the work fulfills you, the rest will come." Yes! THIS is the key to bringing your mindset into the strongest you can achieve. Your mindset will provide a purpose and a mission, and it'll be targeted on that.

Have I enjoyed every part of the journey? Absolutely not! There have been hard times that have been confusing, frustrating, and difficult. However, I've enjoyed most of it and that's why I continued onward. The easiest question you can ask yourself to determine if you're on the right path is, "Would I do this for free?"

Now, don't take this literally, because we all gotta eat! But the point is, if you were in that little surfer town, would you be the woman who said, "This isn't worth it," and shrug it off or would you be the one eager to set up and enjoy the journey?

There's this thing called *"Zero Frequency."* It's a perfect balance in your life to help you achieve peace. But it's also a way of understanding. It's the ability to count your blessings. It's the real you, and where you find your real passion. It's not static, it's clarity and balance. No judgments. Your mind has to reach a state of clarity and focus so you can achieve your goals and be healthy in mind and body. *Zero Frequency* is your goal for your mind so you can reach a sense of peace and harmony within yourself.

How often do you find yourself scrambling around to get to work on time, rushing in, and then having to deal with ridiculously moody coworkers and demanding bosses who stress you out past your breaking point every day? Your everyday life becomes turmoil. Your focus on your goals and aspirations takes a turn you never expected when you were in high school! How do you get off the negative, unfocused life that seems to have grabbed you by the neck and is dragging you away from your purpose in life? It's obviously not an "instant" fix. If it was, you wouldn't see so many of your coworkers and friends in the same career sludge!

There are many life coaches and inspirational speakers out there who confirm who everyone, at some point or another, struggles to find their escape from the grind, the sludge of emptiness. These coaches and speakers sell products to help build your life and career toward a better place. Unfortunately, I honestly think most people who purchase these different programs don't even finish them or even try to use the tools they provide. I'm not putting these speakers or coaches down, in fact I listen to most of them! I'm also not putting down the "unfinishers" of these programs. Instead, I am promoting mindset!

I often listen to Tony Robbins to help get my morning off to a great start. But all that listening can only do so much. These programs can't hold your hand through the process.

We have to want the goal and develop a plan. Just like every other chapter in this book, everything is intertwined. You can be hungry and desperate for success, but having a solid plan to help you achieve it is also required. Otherwise, we'd all be robbing banks and causing whatever mayhem we could get away with in order to chase a dollar!

Apparently, all the goals and planning I implemented made what I did look incredibly easy because every time I turned around, a person at school or someone I ran into at different venues would tell me they'd love to do what I was doing.

There was one girl at the radio station who also did theatre work, and she was convinced that starting a radio show and doing interviews was a piece of cake. I have to be honest here—I was mad as hell. It wasn't just that she wanted to do what I was doing. It was how she thought she could breeze into the radio station and just do it!

By this time, I was around fourteen or fifteen years old and had trudged across Florida, interviewing a few hundred celebrities on location. I hosted a show, spent hours editing audio to send to radio stations, and even more time editing videos to place on YouTube. And on top of all that, I did weekly features of my most recent interviews for the newspaper in New Smyrna Beach, Florida. Trust me, I milked each interview for the maximum footprint I could get out of it!

By the time I finished each week, I was exhausted. And it was only a side hustle from playing steel drum gigs and going to school. It took persistence. It took determination. It took commitment. Yet here was this girl who just waltzed in and thought she could copy my format because it would be "a piece of cake."

As it turned out, she only lasted a few weeks.

I had the mindset, throughout my life, of not just meeting the expectations of my bosses, teachers, parents, and other older people I had to answer to along the way, but to *surpass* those expectations. Quite honestly, I was surprised. Not just in being unique, but also with being the best.

If there was one career I learned the most from, I'd have to say it was being a street performer—a busker. I talked with singer Andy Grammar about his early years, when he was a street performer in California. He agreed how it changes your life. I'm not suggesting you go out and start being a busker, but it does change your life. Perhaps you've done something that was pivotal in how you relate to yourself or think of others in society, such as volunteering at a soup kitchen. There're just moments, frozen in time, when you see how your contribution in society is different than how you earlier thought it would be.

By being a street performer, you're out there all alone. You're at the mercy of someone stopping to listen. If they like what you're performing, maybe they'll throw you a tip, or maybe not. Most people are caught up in their own life moments while passing by you. You're really not on their radar, so you're just there. You hear snippets of conversations, arguments, and then a few curious people ask questions like, "Why are you here?" And, "How old are you?" Most buskers are free spirits, but I was sometimes hired by different businesses that wanted to draw in customers. I'd play for hours, until my fingers were numb, and I could hear the steel drums echo in my head. Even if I wasn't working for a business, I still couldn't take too many breaks, because someone might steal my steel drums. Street performing is, in my experience, the most humbling of jobs I've ever had. It also gets your mind wrapped around your purpose, because if you have no fear of being a street performer, then so many office situations that would embarrass the average person just feel like no big deal to you.

By establishing your mindset to think "good enough isn't really good enough," you are able to push yourself further. You don't take anything for granted. Your eyes and ears are open for any sliver of opportunity that may pass in front of you.

It was my third year in high school when I overheard a rumor about how I was able to get my celebrity interviews because my family was paying for them. You might remember from an earlier chapter how there was also the rumor of my mom working for Lady Gaga. That hurt—a lot. I wondered why someone would think or say something like that. I absolutely never paid, nor did anyone in my family ever pay, for any of the interviews I did. However, I did have a Motown singer who wanted hair and makeup charged to me in order to do the interview, and I refused. I also declined the interview. You need to understand that (even though I still have moments of shaking my head in confusion) the better you do and the more people know about what you do, the more they seem to want to prejudge you or discredit you.

I know I seem to have tough skin now, but in middle and high school I had a monstrous time with being hurt by what people said or thought about me. Maturity has given me the confidence to not concern myself with being underestimated, whether it's for being young or being a female. You have to rise above it.

If the opinions of others impact you so much, you're going to have a really crappy life. Instead, you need to realize it's not relevant to your daily life and you need to just ignore it. Whether it's positive or negative, just go with the flow and don't let the opinions of others influence your life or define your quality of life. On the other hand, you might have to address the lousy person who is making your life hell and call them out on it. Your mindset has to be focused on running the marathon, and you don't need anyone trying to push your buttons. Address the elephant in the room and clarify things, then drop it and move forward. I've found that once people know they can't push you around, they generally take a back seat with their antagonistic attitudes.

Since I've consistently done everything myself—the original one-person band—people typically think there's little I can't do. It's flattering, of course, when I'm at work and someone asks, "Can you do this or that?" I say, "sure." Then I roll my eyes, thinking "Ugh, I did it again!" Two seconds later, after I have my Brittany Spears "I did it again" moment, I recognize I could have said no, and everything still would have been fine. I don't have to be a "yes" woman to be valued within a company. But I do have to value my own worth.

Your mindset needs to withstand so much in today's world. Social media plays a big part. But if you're young, a woman, or a different race, chances are good you've dealt with extra struggles in your professional journey.

Finally, I'm going to throw this out there not to confuse you but to clarify what life really is all about. Millennials and Generation Zers have a hard time, if not an impossible time, understanding how you have everything you need in life—really! God has given you everything you need, and when you become comfortable with this concept, things will come to you because you are at *Zero Frequency* with perfect balance and peace. When you realize you don't need anything, you're able to attract more and attract success. You're able to do this because your mind is clear and focused, and this has you more able to work with clarity, as well as working smarter.

Pavlina's 5 Tips to Strengthen Your Mindset Every Day

1. *Sticky notes to yourself every morning:* Five things you're grateful about.

2. *Cher:* Aww come on! Who can't get excited and want to take on the world (or a snarky co-worker) after listening to Cher blasting out of your speakers?

3. *Facial masks:* They have the power to make you refreshed and feel beautiful in ten minutes!

4. *Your mission:* Have your long-term and short-term goals visible for you to see every day. Get a magnetic calendar for your fridge and gold stars to place on all your successful days.

5. *Your mentor:* Chat with your mentor, whether it's your pastor or anyone who is there to coach you to the next level—someone who understands your struggles.

CHAPTER 8

Plan to Do It and Get It Done

*"Confidence isn't about smoke and mirrors,
or a social media blitz. It's about having the
persistence and fearlessness to be you."*
~ Pavlina Osta ~

I have to say, when I think of confidence, I think of Gene Simmons from KISS. KISS was in Orlando promoting their new football team. I knew nothing about football, but I had heard of KISS. Actually, I didn't even know their songs that well, but I recognized their stage faces. I recognized the brand of KISS. I was going to interview KISS on the red carpet. Media that night was beyond rude, but I managed not to get too many bruises. The handlers brought over Gene Simmons to talk with me, and he called over Paul Stanley, who grudgingly came over as well. Talking to a pre-teen obviously wasn't their priority that evening in order to get maximum coverage for their football team acquisition. Gene played with my name, and the origin of it for a while, then asked if I knew the President of Sweden? Ummm...no. He replied, "Well, most people don't! But, they know KISS!" I later thought this self-confidence was due to a rock-n-roll 70s or 80s persona—sort of an image thing. But a few years later I interviewed Aerosmith's Steven Tyler. He was perfectly cordial and down to earth. One screamed confidence in his brand and status while the other just sort of let you understand it.

Millennials and Generation Zers cautiously approach confidence. It's already shouted at Millennials with their entitlement and overconfidence in the workforce. In reality, we are not a confident set of generations. We admire those with swagger who own their atmosphere, whether that ownership platform is a stage, an office, or just a stroll through a restaurant, with all heads turning. But most Millennials and Generation Zers aren't sure how to get it, and many think you're either born with it or it's unobtainable. If this surprises you, then you're probably someone who falls into the super-confident (with swagger) category.

Millennials are called the therapy generation because they have so many issues, while Gen Zers are two-thirds higher in depression than their predecessors! Most people mistake the Millennials "me, me, me" as selfishness when the majority of it stems from a lack of confidence. Generation Zers are often labeled as smart and savvy. They are the tech generation, and they're also more in tune with global problems than any other generation. They are often organizing protests to fight for the causes they support. It can sometimes be misinterpreted as confidence when, in reality, they're simply trying to hold on to their last strand of hope.

A survey in 2017 reported 33% of Gen Zers indicated they lacked the confidence to lead. Everyone thinks we are so full of ourselves and so overconfident, but it's all a big sham. Like social media, it's all fake. We know it, which is why we get more depressed, because it's like a crazy merry-go-round ride and you can't get off. Society sees Millennials and Gen Zers as inflated asses. I wish it were true, because then at least we'd have the confidence of inflated asses!

Maybe you're one of the few who have confidence and it's not an issue for you. If that is the case, then great for you. This chapter will only reaffirm what you already know. If that's not you, then I hope you'll understand how we are all in this boat together. Huge waves pull us farther out to sea, because we don't know how to stop the feelings we have. We're drowning in our sea of self-doubt. It's almost as if the generations before us are sitting on a nearby boat and staring at us with confusion, as if we put ourselves in this situation.

Have you ever "boohooed" to someone older than you about your life being the worst, only to have them raise their eyebrows, while shaking their head and stating,

"These are supposed to be the best years of your life?" In reality, they are usually the most uncertain and difficult years you will experience.

Why does no one tell you this?

I have no idea! Maybe they don't want to scare you. Or maybe, just maybe, the bouts of sleepless nights, working three jobs, and juggling college courses was so traumatizing to them as well that they stuffed it down deep in the "not worth remembering" part of their memories. I don't know why, but I feel like it has to be mentioned. And since it's fresh on my mind and hasn't been stuffed away in my memory yet, I'm going to do so.

School provides teenagers, and all kids for that matter, a direction and a formula for life. You get up, go to class, study with friends, and repeat it all the next day. Monday through Friday, you're on autopilot. Saturday and Sunday switches to manual mode, where you have to make some decisions. But let's be honest: For the average teen, most of those decisions revolve around chilling out and not thinking too hard. Maybe we mistake it as being similar to adult life. Most appear to have a work routine and chill time, just the same as we did when we were teenagers. Why, then, when we hit that senior year and find ourselves "going out into the world" does it crush over us like a life raft in a tsunami?

I think it's because up to this point, the majority of decisions are being made for us. Even the decisions we as teenagers think are in our court, such as joining a sport or other activity, are actually completely decided and dependent upon someone else. Typically, they are the ones managing all the stress of the decisions—the logistics, the money, or lack thereof, as well as when to move forward and when to back down. We step out of high school and suddenly the consequences of our decisions weigh a lot heavier as we realize every decision we make now falls on us. Oh, and if we mess up, it's not just missing a grade or letting a team down. It could result in losing income, losing resources, or potentially our freedom, depending on how bad we mess things up.

It's no surprise that many of my college friends continued on to graduate school simply because they weren't ready for the real world. For some, it was just the familiarity of the class-to-class and homework routine. But, for others, it was the inability to venture too far away from the safety of their parents. Really, for all of them, it was a lack of confidence. There were some who played it off cool and said things like, "Graduate school will give me an edge in the job market," even though they had no vision or plan as to what they'd pursue. I often had to make myself think of roadkill during these conversations simply to keep myself from breaking out in laughter. Wouldn't knowing what market you wanted to apply in give you the most "edge" to start with anyway?

Of course, since we *are* the tech generations, it would be remiss of me to not bring in social media's role. We post enticing pictures intended to have people wishing they had our lives or, at the very least, be on our dream vacation. There is so much great escapism happening on a daily basis over social media. The person who is laughing at a football game while you're at home watching Netflix? You don't realize how they're drowning in debt, just like you, because they charge every single vacation just to keep up their "life is good" act. The person posting inspirational quotes and always smiling while you're bawling under the covers as you look at one more quote hoping it will help? They've been battling so much anxiety and depression that they've turned to drugs as an outlet to cope. Is that always the case? No. Is it sometimes the case? Yes.

My point is that confidence is never something you can gain by comparing yourself to others. Facebook is for looking friends up, not looking at them! When I post stuff on social media, I'm never trying to put out an image that I have it all together or anyone should try to keep up with me. I post because I enjoyed something and wanted to share that joy with others in my life. When I view stuff on social media, I do so because I find it fascinating, entertaining, or informative. I want to see what others are doing not so I can compete, but to stay connected and know what's happening in their lives.

So, in review, as twenty-somethings we lack confidence, largely due to the fact that up to this point we have lacked any real responsibility, along with our constant need to compare and measure up to others. As for women, there's also the third strike, as I mentioned in Chapter 1, from the pressures presented by society that make them feel "less than" men.

That was a lot to take in. I realize that. But it was important to go through the major things that cause the lack of confidence so we can better understand how to build up our confidence moving forward.

1. **Recognize your fear and step up to it now!**
   When we fear something, we want to avoid it. We decide to do it tomorrow or simply not at all. Don't delay! Start today by identifying your goals and creating a plan to achieve them. Be committed.

2. **Learn to lead**
   Write down your worth. Have a mentor help you with this. Then start viewing yourself as valuable and important. You don't have to have it all together, or know it all, to bring a presence to a room. You simply have to look professional and know who you are.

3. **Read the room**

I learned this early at networking events. There are always people at an event who you want to know and others who are probably a waste of your time. Get to the key players and then move to the less crucial contacts. Also, feel the vibe of the room in order to morph your personality accordingly.

4. **Stand out by being assertive**

Remember my story about attending an event in Florida? There were so many times when I was typically mistaken for a school kid who had won backstage passes as I was approaching someone to conduct an interview, even with my camera gear and media credentials! I didn't have time to explain myself at every security stop. I had to learn to walk into the event like I was Barbara Walters or I'd get lost in the shuffle. People typically stand up and pay attention when you understand your role and wear it with confidence.

5. **Learn to say no**

When you understand who you are and stand on that, life is no longer about people-pleasing or self-promoting. You're not wandering around, saying yes to everything, so you can achieve the cheers of others. And you're not saying yes to ensure you advance. When you know who you are, you're able to say "no," without guilt, to all the things that don't align with who you are and where you're going. This is not a selfish act, as some may misjudge it to be. Instead, it is an act of self-awareness we would all be so much better off embracing.

6. **Learn to collaborate**

Collaborations can be life savers. You learn/they learn. Collaborations come in all sizes and shapes, but the important way they help your confidence is how you learn to embrace your strengths and weaknesses. This can then save you time and stress. When you allow someone else to contribute their strength, which is vastly different from your strength, you'll find yourself more secure with your own insecurities. Why stress over your weaknesses when you can collaborate with someone who balances you out?

7. **Confront troublemakers**

There's always that person who wants to discredit you in front of the boss and throw you under the bus. And when they catch your look of shock or irritation, they do the "hands up" in front of an "innocent face" while shrugging their shoulders and asking, "What?" There were moments when I turned snarky on those types of people after dealing with their attitude longer than I ever should have allowed. And I'm not a snarky person at all. While sometimes painful, I found that confronting them stopped the hemorrhage of wasted hours agonizing and making myself miserable. On other occasions, I confronted their trouble-making without saying a word to their face. Instead, I did such a great job that they were left with nothing to criticize or no one to believe their claims. Either way, confronting the enemy in person or dazzling them with your talent will raise your confidence level a good notch or two higher!

8. **Cut negative people out of your life**

These can be the obvious negative people who cut you down, or they can be friends who, for some reason, make you feel down in the dumps after a conversation with them. It's important to identify them and limit your contact with them. The less they are around, the less influence they'll have on you. Opportunities and positive thinking can't happen with these negative people around you.

9. **Be kind to others**

Mister Rogers once said, "There are three ways to ultimate success: The first way is to be kind. The second way is to be kind. The third way is to be kind."

When I've been kind to other people, I have found it gave me a sense of confidence. Even if it was only something simple, such as helping a lady get her baby stroller up the steps from the subway station. Knowing I helped someone gave me a confidence boost. Being of service to someone else takes your self-worth up a notch!

10. Start the day positive!

Positive thoughts and feelings give you confidence. I wake up, turn on my fragrance machine, and crank out a great song to listen to while I get dressed in my Lululemons and go to exercise class. By the time I go into my office, I'm ready to take on the world—and any grumpy person around me!

Like I mentioned at the beginning of this chapter, most of us believe confidence is either something you have, or you don't. You're born with it or you're not, and there's no way to obtain it. I was not born with confidence, but I can confirm there are moments and times when I am totally confident. There might be some people who are born with confidence, but the reality for most of us is that we are simply faking it until we make it. There were situations when I had to display confidence or I would have been drowned out in my industry. Did it suggest I was confident in the moment or in the outcome? Not so much, but I had to be sure of who I was to survive it! Why? Because your opportunity sometimes needs a little push.

The best personal example I can give of confidence is when, at ten years old, I interviewed Kevin Jonas. It wasn't easy.

It was on world-famous Daytona Beach at the iconic *Bandshell*, which was to host Kevin Jonas and a variety of performers. Everyone was excited about the front-page news event. Daytona Beach was finally going to be more than home of NASCAR and crazy spring breakers. I didn't read the papers, because what ten-year-old would? But the buzz around my school was intense and kids were skipping school in order to stand in line for a meet-and-greet with Kevin Jonas.

I, however, wasn't going to do it. I've never been a fan girl, except for Oprah. But I thought I'd cover the event, and screaming girls can be interesting to interview. I get to the *Bandshell* and find an up-and-coming singer who's an opening act to interview at the Hilton. After finishing the interview, I leave the hotel, which is next door to the *Bandshell*, and I see a huge crowd gathered for Kevin Jonas. The venue is a plaza with shops and restaurants. A girl I know spots me and waves at me from the ice cream shop where she's working. She begins telling me the crowd has been waiting for hours, some overnight, so they can get into the meet-and-greet with Kevin Jonas, which was being conducted upstairs near the movie theater.

As she's continuing on about how unbelievable the hype of the whole thing is, I suddenly have an idea. I thanked the girl and pushed myself into the line of screaming kids.

Like a sheep, I followed along, blending in with the rest of the herd. There were no wristbands or stamps that identified you as a recipient of the meet-and-greet. It was one of the most unorganized and craziest events I have been involved in, and I'm actually thankful it was so chaotic! It allowed me to be escorted all the way to the meet-and-greet, where Kevin Jonas's manager, Johnny Wright, was monitoring the entire process. When I realized he was the man in charge, I told him, "I'm here to interview Kevin Jonas."

He looked at me with raised eyebrows, "Oh you are?" He asked as he sized up my four-foot-tall frame, with me looking just like one of the crazed fans. Maybe it was my camera, Sony recorder, and steno pad that helped set me apart, although I'm not sure. I'd like to think it was my confidence in knowing who I was and what I was there to do that made Mr. Wright smile and reply, "Okay, sure."

This interview carried a lot of importance to me. I was prepared to do whatever it took at that moment to get it done so my radio show would not just be good, but great. I'm not naturally an outgoing, vivacious, or assertive person. I was always the quiet one in the classroom. But outside of class, when I was doing my radio work, I was surprisingly assertive. No didn't mean "no" to me—it meant I had to find another technique to turn it to a "maybe" or a "yes."

After the Jonas interview, I walked down the stairs and saw a veteran newspaper editor leaning against a pillar. I knew him from my steel drum performances because he had interviewed me for a story earlier that year. We greeted each other and he asked what I was doing. I mentioned I just wrapped up interviewing Kevin Jonas upstairs. His face was in total disbelief, so I shared the camera and recording with him. He couldn't get an interview with Jonas and asked how I managed to do so. I told him and he just nodded. Like I said in Chapter 1, stop using your age as an excuse—it is a gift. People don't expect much from young people, but young people with confidence can often make things happen.

When I began doing on-location interviews with Sean Hannity in New York City, I mentioned the Kevin Jonas interview and he told me he was surprised I wasn't arrested. Honestly, if I had been escorted off the premises, I would have found another way back into the event. I was so determined to make that interview happen. That's really the mindset and level of courage you need to have if you want something bad enough. The confidence comes when you have a chorus of voices in your head chanting, "You got this—you can do it!"

One of the most confident and energetic people I met was TV fitness personality Tony Little. I've interviewed more than 600 celebrities, and probably just as many non-celebrities, so I'd like to think I can accurately tell real people from fake people. With that being said, Tony Little is the real deal. He's just as dynamic, motivated, and caring in real life as he is in his infomercials. He's compassionate, loves what he does, and is very successful with it. Plus, he's just so enthusiastic!

In the interview, I asked Tony, "How did you get confident? What's your best formula for being confident and staying confident?"

He replied, "Ultimately, your confidence may not be at 100% all the time, but you can achieve it by making a few changes in your life. What it does need is consistency with your effort, and that's best monitored with a 30-day calendar. Because once you form a habit of consistency with your confidence, the permanence will be more stabilized."

CHAPTER 9

Be Brave

"Courage is not the absence of fear, but
the action in the presence of it."
~ Mark Twain ~

Courage is not something obvious to all of us. Millennials and Gen Zers especially think of courage and dismiss it as a hologram. Most people don't feel courageous to these generations. Sure, there's the firefighter one hears about on the news, rescuing people from a burning building. There's the underdog who stands up for some environmental issue and it goes viral. But we don't look for heroes and we certainly don't see ourselves as courageous. However, I think most people are extremely courageous. They just don't recognize it in themselves. When you start recognizing it, though, you'll start having more self-worth and more confidence in yourself!

I remember watching *Courage the Cowardly Dog* for the first time when I was seven or eight years old. The cartoon originally aired on Nickelodeon from 1996-2002, so by the time I was introduced to it, they were all reruns. I remember, at the time, that I found Courage to be the most unlikely courageous dog imaginable! He was scared of everything. Chickens scared him, aliens scared him, the abusive husband of Mural especially scared him. How could he be named Courage?

When I was younger, all I could think about while watching that cartoon was the fear Courage showed. It was just silly how a dog named Courage was so afraid of everything. Obviously, the owners had no idea how to name their pet.

Now that I'm older, I can see how the writers used this as an attention-getter. Courage the Cowardly Dog. How can you use *courage* and *cowardly* to describe the same character? Wouldn't that be inaccurate? Actually, it's right on point. This anthropomorphic dog is an excellent reflection of the average person.

No one ever labels Courage as a hero. He's afraid of everything, which makes him cowardly. But without fail, he always does something to help save the day. He never seeks to be the hero. At the end of the episode, he takes joy in knowing Mural was spared from harm. That is the only reason he does what he does to save the day because he thinks more of Mural than he does of himself.

All too often, we fail to see ourselves as courageous.

I remember my first courageous moment. I was playing my steel drums on the beach. It was January and there were maybe ten people on the beach: a few couples, a determined surfer, an occasional jogger, and some snowbirds who actually thought sixty degrees was warm. I had lugged my big, double seconds steel drums down to the beach and started playing. I knew about three or four songs and just repeated them over and over again for the next few hours. Some people stopped and listened. Most gave me a side look and continued on the beach. While I was playing, about ten feet away, there was an old guy making crosses out of palm fronds. We would talk between songs. At the end of the day, when I was putting the stands and drums away, the old man gave me some advice, and I'll never forget the advice he gave me that day.

He told me I should go to the management at Ocean Plaza and ask to play in front of one of the stores. He said he'd seen other buskers in front of the Starbucks and said I had a good chance of being there. I asked him why he wasn't there. The Ocean Plaza Shoppes were by the *Bandshell*. The shop area was covered and had a good amount of people coming and going. The old man shook his head and explained he wasn't allowed up there. I guessed he was homeless, but I didn't ask. We talked for a little bit longer and then went our separate ways. The following week, I was set up in front of Starbucks at the Ocean Plaza Shoppes. I looked for the old man down on the beach. I wanted to thank him for his advice, but he was nowhere to be found and I never saw him again.

I never gave it much thought, but looking back, I can see it took courage to be a busker on the beach. It took courage to talk with an old person who looked to be homeless. He could have been an ax murderer or child molester—I wouldn't have known! It took courage to go into the management office and ask if I could perform in front of their shops. At the time, I didn't see it as unusual or brave, but in reality it wasn't easy to do. It definitely took courage to perform in the heavily-trafficked space in front of Starbucks. Kids asked why I was there, and lots of people gave me all kinds of different looks while others just ignored me. But I continued and never considered it courageous.

Oftentimes, we overlook our courageous moments because we're just going through the motions of the moment. Nothing seems extraordinary to us because we're just living our day. It is typically other people who pick up on our courage long before we ever realize we possess it. That was the case when I was approached by the owner of the biggest—and only—water park in Daytona Beach. The park was located across the street from the Starbucks where I played. No doubt he had heard me perform on quite a few occasions. When he approached me, he asked if I could play the steel drums at the water park after the spring breakers left. I didn't know when they would leave, but I said sure. It turned out the water park owner wanted me there after April, which was when the water park business went in to full swing. I went from playing on the beach with an audience of ten to playing in front of Starbucks with quite a bit more traffic, and finally playing at a fully packed water park!

Not only do we fail to recognize our own acts of courage, but we also fail to define our own self-worth from any of these acts. While I didn't feel scared during my early street performances, I did feel vulnerable. My lack of fear may have been instilled in me during my time with competitive dance. You practice, you perform, and you think very little about any of the other details. You simply show up and do what you've planned to do. But unlike my time with competitive dance where there were peers, teachers, judges, and a whole host of other people, as a busker I was on my own.

It is in those moments when we have no one else around to support us or encourage us that we have to stir up some courage to get ourselves through things. Here are some ways to recognize and strengthen your courage.

1. **Overcome that fear**

   Unless it's a physical fear, such as being threatened at gunpoint, it is easy to recognize the root cause of most of our fears being the inability to get out of our comfort zones. Fear, like stress, can be harmful for us, so get over it! Don't watch all your hard work result in nothing because of a fear that only has power when you empower it.

2. **Clear your headspace**

   Whether it is exercising, yoga, meditation, or journaling, find an outlet to help keep your headspace clear. Daily exercise makes such a difference in my life. I always feel the difference if I don't take time to exercise. I feel blah, unfocused, and generally let things bother me more if I've not exercised. Exercise strengthens my body. It also wraps me in a strong shield of power. I know others find this through journaling or meditation, or a combination of multiple outlets. Implementing ways of clearing your headspace is a major way of strengthening your courage.

3. **Do a thirty-day calendar**

   I have one of those magnetic calendars in my apartment. When I want a useful trait to become a habit, I fill in the month with a sharpie, get my gold star stickers (teachers love me for remembering my days of achieving rows of gold stars in the classroom!) and give myself a gold star each day I fulfill a goal. This may seem like a silly thing to do to grow courage. But courage is like any other muscle, it needs repetitive workouts to grow. Implementing a thirty-day calendar brings the discipline needed to help strengthen courage.

4. **Be a turtle**

   Slow and steady is the way to go. If you're afraid of talking to people, then attending a packed-out event shouldn't be at the top of your list as one of the first things to do to build up your courage. Start with arranging more one-on-one meetings than you typically would, then attend a few small events and challenge yourself to talk to a set number of people while you're there. Maybe that number is only three to start, and that's okay. Just do it. Go at it gradually to help ensure success.

5. **Breathe**
Yeah, this is pretty obvious. It's something we have to do to live. But trust me, when you're feeling scared or anxious, this is a great technique to build your courage. Right before I go on the air, or head onto a stage for a speaking engagement, I take some deep breaths and focus on my topics, replaying certain parts in my head. Fear will speed up our heart rate and take over the show if we allow it. This presents itself as panic attacks or nervous breakdowns—the frozen deer caught in headlights mindset. By taking deep breaths, we can take control of our body. Mentally walking through what will be required of us, and seeing ourselves succeed, allows us to show courage when the moment comes, no matter the task.

6. **Accept failures**
You prepared for it, you tried, and the end result still wasn't up to par with how you wanted it to go. That's okay. There's tomorrow. There's another opportunity.

If you gave it your best, then be proud of it. If you have to admit you only gave it a half-assed go, then own up to it and give it your best next time. There's no point in crumbling to pieces over it. Accept what you need to learn from the situation, then continue onward. It will make you even stronger for the next moment.

7. **Give your thoughts voice**

Most of us lack courage because there are a million voices inside our heads telling us how big a coward we happen to be. When you do something courageous, even if it is a little thing, congratulate yourself. "Hey, I rode the subway by myself and I survived!" Also, don't be afraid to verbally shut up the negative voices by saying, "I can do this!" You might save this action for moments when you're by yourself, unless you find padded walls appealing, but make sure you do it. When you think, *I'm going to totally flop that thing tomorrow,"* verbally reply, "No, I am not! I am going to do really well because I have practiced and planned, and I'm prepared!" You'll be amazed at how quickly your confidence grows. After all, let's be honest, we typically have the best opinion about our opinion.

8. **Stop overthinking**

This is my biggest pitfall! Courage is like a helium balloon. The longer you wait, the less balloon you have to work with at a particular time. Don't wait for everything to be perfect because you'll wait forever and never take any steps out of your comfort zone. Start right away and then take gradual steps you can ease into. Don't procrastinate and don't delay. You're avoiding the situation and you know it. Think of Courage the Cowardly Dog. He's unsure, but that doesn't stop him from doing what he knows has to be done. Overthinking stalls and crushes your desire to carry through on something. As Nike says, "Just do it."

Our deepest fears and vulnerabilities can stop us from pursuing our dreams. Having courage and addressing our fears, weaknesses, pains, and vulnerabilities can be a tough thing to do. Social media has become, for many, a therapy platform to help navigate our fears. I've seen long narratives on Facebook from friends explaining their depression and the struggle they live with in trying to overcome it. I saw a friend discussing his coming out and the prejudices he has to navigate in his personal and professional career.

Shaquille O'Neal once told me his biggest obstacles were marijuana and knives. He said it took courage to say no and stay one step ahead of his peers and neighborhood influences. Shaq understood, at an early age, the importance of establishing boundaries in order to save himself from personal or professional harm. I doubt if he labeled himself courageous, but he did know his self-worth and developed confidence by establishing his boundaries. That gave him the byproduct known as respect.

Maybe you're thinking, "Yes, but he is Shaquille O'Neal!" It's easy to discredit someone as courageous when, by the time we learn about them, they are successful and doing well. That brings me to another celebrity with a different twist on their story.

I've interviewed some of the biggest boy bands. It's always a fun time because boy bands are high energy and sometimes a little flirty. We all know that's what the audience wants to see, and I would go along with it. The courageous celebrity who comes to mind is Aaron Carter, younger brother of Nick Carter, who is best known as one of the Backstreet Boys. Aaron achieved a celebrity persona that most sibling performers only hope to achieve—to be as popular as their older sibling. The first time I interviewed Aaron was at a hotel in Orlando. He had just given a performance for a small group of a hundred or so screaming, totally smitten teenaged girls. Well, on stage he was a successful solo singer, performer, and heartthrob to fans. But backstage in the interview, Aaron was a little shy, very nice, and exceptionally polite. I thought, "Wow! He's so sweet!"

A few years later we did another interview. At that time, he had changed public relations companies, and it wasn't as organized as the first interview. When I got to the venue, which was a grungy, hole-in-the-wall kind of bar, I had to wait, uncomfortably, for about twenty minutes or so while being thoroughly freaked out. I didn't blend in well, being a sixteen-year-old in a neon pink puffer vest, so the looks and stares were making me very uncomfortable.

I was finally brought back to do the interview and the tour manager walked into the tour bus first, guiding me on where to set up my camera. But, the Aaron in this interview felt like a completely different person. His joy was gone, his face was thinner, and honestly I felt uncomfortable on the tour bus. I've talked with a lot of celebrities on their tour buses, so it wasn't that I didn't feel comfortable with the setting. It just felt off. This was in 2014.

The venues he was performing at were getting smaller and smaller, but here he was, still chugging right along. You probably read through all this and wonder why I want to label Aaron Carter as someone who had courage. For me, Aaron, like Courage the Cowardly Dog, could be overlooked. He isn't seen as doing anything special because he is a performer who, at the time, was still performing. But for me he showed courage because despite personal pain he was struggling to overcome, he was still carrying onward.

Courage is something we all have in our minds and souls. Most of us just don't realize it. It is the determination to overcome the fear. The key is to recognize your courage, and understand your self-doubt and vulnerabilities. When you do so, the courage will manifest for you. This isn't your magic formula for being courageous, because I'm insisting there isn't one. There isn't one because you already have courage inside you. The magic is to recognize it and feel your self-worth because of it. Realize that everyone is afraid of something, but the difference is how you deal with your fear.

Our courage has to be in place because there will be places and times it will be needed. As Winston Churchill said, "Nothing in life is so exhilarating as to be shot at without result."

CHAPTER 10

You've Had It All Along!

"Your purpose in life is to find your purpose
and give your whole heart and soul to it."
~ Buddha ~

If you have found your purpose, you're one of the lucky few. I have met so many people who have no direction. I thought, sure, in high school no one really knows what they want to do and, to be honest, everyone changes their minds and their degree majors a few times during college. So, what's the big deal? Millennials do worry about this and that's one of the big deals! Our twenty-something minds want a purpose, but we also want a paycheck! In fact, we have to have the paycheck to live. So, Millennials and Gen Zers think about chasing the dollar, just like the generations preceding them, which is who they hate to emulate in any way whatsoever!

Back in the day, the so-called American Dream was defined as follows: finish high school, get a college degree, get married, start a family, and settle down in a house in the suburbs where you'll still be living late into your sixties. The purpose of all these things was simple—security. Life and security have new implications today and the

American Dream has been redefined. Therefore, twenty-somethings have no desire to slave away for a company, obtain a coveted, gold-plated watch for twenty-five years of service, and then retire with a pension plan. Life passes you by when you live like that.

It's a difficult thing to balance. Millennials want job security, but without a feeling of purpose they are discontent. Gen Zers are even more driven to choose purpose as their priority over a paycheck. Unfortunately, most people who exit high school without a clear purpose for their life end up throwing any hope for it out the window. School debt, everyday bills, and the simple costs of living begin to weigh them down. So, "purpose" is written off as a quality only some people possess, but not them.

Finding your purpose early in life used to be so easy. My first-grade teacher asked what I wanted to be when I grew up. My answer was dancer. My fourth-grade teacher asked what I wanted to be when I grew up. My answer was Broadway dancer. I was convinced I'd be a dancer in New York City. Life changes, I changed, and other opportunities came my way. But it felt strange at first to no longer be saying, "I am going to be a dancer."

That passion, and what I thought to be my purpose at the time, was being replaced by a new interest, and a surprising gift I had, of talking to people. So, for whatever reason, people were comfortable when they talked to me.

When I asked something out of curiosity, they'd feel comfortable answering my question. It was almost as if they sensed it was just a question and not a ploy to create a sensational headline.

I interviewed Florida Governor Charlie Crist back when he was running for the United States Senate. Florida is a strange state when it comes to politics, and Governor Crist was having a rough time. I had already interviewed one candidate in Daytona Beach, and I was in Tallahassee as a Page for Representative Dwayne Taylor. I had a few questions for Governor Crist and finished by asking him to tell me his favorite Broadway show. The randomness of the question shook him a little, but he recovered and said, "*West Side Story*." The next day, I took a tour of the Florida Governor's mansion, and it was known I had interviewed Governor Crist. The assistant at the mansion wondered why I hadn't asked Governor Crist the "million-dollar question." I'm sure I looked perplexed. I don't know what the "million-dollar question" was supposed to be, but mine had already been answered, regarding his favorite Broadway show. At the time, I had my sights set on Broadway, so that answer was of most importance to me.

I didn't realize how fortunate I'd been to find my gift early in my career until my first year in college, when it was easy to see how many of my friends had no idea what they were doing. That made no sense to me. They were going to college and really had very little idea where they wanted to go, or how they would get there once they decided.

Finding your purpose, to some people, sounds like a daunting and unobtainable task. Some people refuse to take the time to discover it because they're afraid they'll turn up purposeless. Maybe that's because we often mash together purpose and talent. If you are talented at basketball, then your purpose must be to play professionally, or teach or coach. So, when something happens like an injury, then those individuals find themselves lacking purpose. No, purpose is much deeper than a mere talent.

Your purpose is best defined as this: It is something you believe in. Something that holds you in awe. Something that makes you proud. In reality, your purpose is *you*. But it also doesn't completely define you. It is something buried so deep inside you that it often takes some time before you really discover what it is.

I was a great ballerina. I loved ballet and I was good at ballet, but there was something developing in the background of which I was unaware. Your purpose won't be something that will benefit you alone. It will be something that allows you to be of benefit to others as well.

Today, Gloria Steinem is known as an iconic feminist, social political activist, and author, but she wasn't always a powerhouse for feminism. In fact, I'm not even sure it was ever her intention to be seen as a rebel. She saw a need and ran to fill it. Her gift to be the voice for women's equality was established, and her purpose was, at that time, formed.

I was sixteen years old when I had the chance to interview her. I was expecting a hard-lined, impatient, get-to-the-facts female, but that's not who I met that day. She was empathetic to young women, and soft spoken. Even though she was tired after arriving from the airport and going straight to the hotel for our interview, she never showed it. And although she'd be leaving our interview to give a speech at an abortion clinic across the street, you'd never have known it from our time together. She treated me like I was the only one on her schedule that day. Her parting words as we exited the hotel lobby were, "Keep up what you're doing. You're on the right track."

Your purpose isn't necessarily your passion, but your purpose does involve your gift. Oftentimes, others will pick up on your purpose quickly, such as the friends who recognize and say, "You're a really good listener." Or subtle comments like, "I wish I was as patient as you." These may not seem like they indicate a purpose, but take note because there is something more to them than empty comments. Your purpose is something you are naturally good at. You might not think your natural talent will make you money or be something you can make into a career, but it can, and it will! First, I'll explain some ways to find your purpose. Many claim your purpose is your passion, but I'm an advocate of focusing on finding your gift because that's how you'll discover your purpose!

1. **Where's your easy button?**

   What are you are most comfortable about? What comes easiest for you? It doesn't have to be complicated stuff. Maybe it's easy for you to remain calm while your friends quickly melt down. Maybe keeping things organized seems like a no-brainer. You are so used to these things you don't even realize how not everyone possesses them.

2. **Do what you love**

   Think about what makes you happy. I've been told this over and over by celebrities and entrepreneurs: You have to love what you do. Discover what makes you happy and the pay will follow. Everything follows once you put into place the natural talent you reveal and focus on it. You love working on it and your passion with it will push you to your success.

3. **What energizes you?**

   Every time I get in front of the mic or camera, I get energized. Everything else—just having a bad day overall, grumpy people, having no milk in the fridge—all of it fades away when I start to talk about an issue for my show. That's how I know it's a passion.

4. **Would you do it for free?**

   Remember the story I mentioned about performing with my steel drums in New Smyrna Beach and the performer who was leaving as I was getting ready to start my performance? She couldn't see the worth in performing for nothing. We all want to be paid for our talents and our labors, but would you still do it if you had to do it for free? We all need money to pay our bills, but you'll never be happy doing a job that doesn't utilize your gifts in some way.

5. **Start goal-setting in order to reach your destination**

   I've set a lot of goals over my lifetime. Some were achieved and some were not. Achieving at least one Guinness World Record by the time I was eighteen years old was one of my goals. My first world record was something I knew doing blindfolded, even with a book of rules attached to it, which was interviewing people! Another goal I had was to be working in New York City before I was eighteen years old. I don't know why age eighteen was such a magic number to me, but it was important that I achieved landmark career objectives by that age. I visualized each of these things happening, and by constantly having the vision in front of me, as well as working toward the goals, I managed some impressive early achievements. Goal-setting and visualization is like GPS for your purpose. It makes a big difference when you map out your long-term and short-term goals, as well as your daily objectives.

6. **Know where you're going**

Where do you want to be next year? In five years? Be present in the future by the way you dress and act. I always stepped into a venue defined by who I was as a person. Not suits, not prissy pastel dresses, but a strong sense of style—that was me. Doc Martens, vintage Escada blazers, graphic tees, and a Gucci belt. Yes, I could dial it back and wear a newscaster's navy blue dress with nude, three-inch pumps that screamed traditional Calvin Klein. But that's not where I wanted to be in five years. Imagine where you want to be in the future. Remember Imagine Dragons' Dan Reynolds' image board I mentioned earlier? Imagery is a powerful tool. It can be a useless tool, though, if it's not combined with strategy. Don't just see yourself somewhere, like the people who covet being a famous singer but do nothing to make it happen. There's a lot of strategy and work that happens between thinking of being a singer and stepping onto a stage to a screaming audience! Knowing what you want and setting a plan to achieve it is imperative.

7. **Where and when are you the happiest?**

Is it when you're baking? When you travel? Working on different crafts or activities? It always amazes me there are so many people who think their most extreme, happiest moments are only that and nothing more. They don't think it's possible to take the hobby up a notch and make it a career. It's very possible, even probable, and it will make you the happiest career person you know! Why would you not take that chance and reach for it?

8. **Relax**

Your mind, soul, and body need time to relax. We can't contemplate the future when we're stressed out. It's a matter of reaching a state of mind where you can visualize peace and love. If you aren't able to find this peace within yourself, then the need to fill your purpose is going to seem challenged. I went to Costa Rica for a yoga retreat with a bunch of yoga gurus, mainly from the Washington DC area. They were people I'd never met. I was simply hoping for a relaxing time with yoga enthusiasts like myself. But I actually ended up forming lifelong friendships and continued with annual yoga retreat excursions. The trip was amazing and it provided me a whole new insight into my wellbeing. It formed internal guidance for myself, and journaling helped me to get all the junk and confusion out of my head. So, I highly recommend yoga, meditation, and journaling to help you keep your shit together and clarify what's in your brain.

9. **Talk to someone you trust**

   Sometimes we're too close to what's going on around us and we simply cannot see what we have to work with as our gifts. We may not see ourselves as great at anything, or at least not something we can turn into a career. But someone else who knows you will be able to see your talent, even if you do not.

Your gift is special, and it deserves your attention. Make the effort, be bold and take the chance, because as John Quincy Adams said, "Try and fail, but don't fail to try."

I was interviewing singer/songwriter Jack Johnson at the Amway Center in Orlando, and he explained how he got into music. It wasn't when he was younger. He had a surfing accident and was injured. During his time in the hospital, he was bored. A friend suggested playing the guitar, and that's how it all began! Jack is a casual, soft-spoken, calm person—very different from most of the musicians I talk with, who are so full of energy. After our interview, we left the VIP area and Jack gave me a tour of the arena. The ground level contained a dozen or so non-profit tables related to helping the environment. His own special project at the time was reusing plastic water bottles and promoting plastic-free alternatives. This was back in 2010, so he was at the beginning of a new movement. He had taken his gift of music and combined it with his love for the environment.

Jack is the perfect example, in my opinion, of someone who found his gift, enjoys his gift, and has allowed the gift to springboard into other fantastic endeavors.

Establishing your purpose can take a lot of anxiety out of your life. Remember the old homeless man I met while I was playing steel drums in New Smyrna Beach? He encouraged me to play in a heavier-traffic area, and that opened up other opportunities for me. But the more important advice he gave to me was right before we parted. He told me to love what I do, because it will make all the difference. Don't chase fame. Don't chase the money or the social media followers. Chase what you love to do, because the rest will follow.

My life moves so fast that sometimes, being the average Generation Z girl, I forget to stop and think about things that have happened around me. Sometimes, I don't realize until months afterward, or even years later, the impact a particular person or event had on my life. That old man on the beach was one of those moments. It was an extremely odd coincidence how we met that day, because I never saw him again. He was an old man, making crosses out of palm fronds. I don't remember him making any sales with his craft. Maybe I'm a little fanciful, but I believe he was there for me, like an angel. He was a guiding figure for me.

Maybe you don't have a guiding figure around you. Maybe you have a lot of insecurity. Maybe you're not sure if your gift can turn into a serious career. I say *maybe* because I think everyone has at least a hunch about what they are good at. But we all hope to have someone who will reassure us of it. We all think we should be more confident if we truly are good at something. In the entrepreneurship-type of strong world we live in today, we're certainly all hopeful our gifts will allow us to strike outside the box and see our talents flourish into successful careers.

This entire chapter can be summed up using my younger sister as an example. She had no idea what she wanted to do all through secondary school. She went to dance with me, but never liked it. She tolerated gymnastics, until she saw a girl break her jaw on the uneven bars. There was no school sport she liked, nor was there a subject in school she liked more than any other. I imagine she felt, as so many of us have at one time or another, purposeless. There was no evidence of anything she seemed to be truly passionate about.

Then came the day she decided to redecorate her bedroom. Her bedroom had previously been occupied by our older sister, who had since moved out. From our point of view, the bedroom my mom and older sister had decorated was already magazine-perfect. So, when Fiona began her redecorating, the rest of the family didn't know what to expect. Most of us imagined it'd turn out black and pink, with posters on the walls, or something equally repugnant. We wanted to encourage her creativity, but couldn't help but cringe at having no idea what her personality would unveil.

A week later, she came back to us to discuss her ideas. She had color swatches from Home Depot, pictures of accessories from Marshalls on her phone, and some ideas on a makeover for the overcrowded closet. I think we all had our mouths hanging open in disbelief when she finished explaining and describing it all. A few months later, her room was transformed, and we all agreed it was great.

Through this simple task she took upon for herself, she found her purpose. The following summer, Fiona did a short session at one of the NYC interior design schools. She loved it!

Your purpose is worth pursuing and worth taking a risk to achieve. It's the most important part of your future and will help you carve out your success. The love you have for your gift will sustain you through difficult and endless hours of making your mark in the world. Your confidence in your ability will come into play, as well as your courage to make it happen.

Have faith in yourself and it will all work out just fine!

CHAPTER 11

Accept to Expect the Unexpected: How to Overcome Obstacles

"Fall seven times, stand up eight."
(Japanese proverb)

When I first started my interviews, the ability to overcome obstacles fascinated me. Throughout my tween and teenage years, I had seen many students in my dance and gymnastics classes struggle constantly, myself being one of them. There were the normal struggles with vying for a particular dance part. Then there were injury struggles, and personalities to shrug off. There were also struggles with body weight and personal appearance that were fairly normal obstacles for athletic people. So, these struggles bounced through my mind while preparing questions for interviews. How did these celebrities rise above everything? What were their obstacles? How did they overcome them?

The more interviews I conducted, the more I realized how obstacles took on a whole new perspective with age and experience. The older the person, the less they considered anything a "real obstacle." As an example, my grandmother wasn't a celebrity or a newsmaker. She grew up during The Great Depression and WWII. As if those weren't big enough challenges, she had many daily obstacles. For school, she walked two miles to get there every day, regardless of the weather. As a farm girl in Ohio, this required walking in snowstorms—by herself. There was no money in her home because of The Great Depression. Taking a bath consisted of using a metal tub in the kitchen, behind the stove.

She took care of her mother until her mom died. After her mom's death, she was informed the farm was willed to her older brother, who promptly sold it, thus leaving her homeless. She got married just to have a roof over her head. Talk about obstacles! I can't even imagine having to live through a fraction of her life. But when grandma talked about those years, it was all just part of her life. It was not extraordinary or troubled, it was just there.

Some people have passion and purpose that helps drive them through the obstacles they face. For some people, life itself is the only fuel they need to push through their obstacles. Just keep living! We will all face obstacles and experience setbacks, but we can't allow these to detour us from achieving our goals.

While interviewing singer-songwriter Jack Johnson, I learned he had a surfing accident when he was seventeen years old. The surfboard hit his face hard enough that it required 150 stitches in his forehead and lip, as well as some fake teeth in the front. He went on to say he was a little bit worried about the whole thing. He wasn't sure if he was going to be able to surf like before because fear from the accident felt ever-present. How did he overcome his obstacle?

"I just learned to slowly push myself, in a comfortable way, back to the same place I was before I had the accident. But that was definitely one of those times I wasn't sure I was going to be able to do the thing I loved at the same level. I think, just by persevering and continuing to try as best I could, I got back to the place I was before" (from Jack Johnson Interview w/ Pavlina).

Overcoming obstacles collaborates with your inner strength and courage to yield a positive goal for yourself. Just like the Japanese proverb at the beginning of this chapter, there's a passage in the Bible which is similar,

> "Though a righteous man falls seven times, he
> will get up but the wicked will stumble into ruin."
> ~ Proverbs 24:16 ~

My summary of these quote would be this: "As the good and strong person you are, you will succeed and find your heart's desire."

Whatever is in your life driving you, you'll find the means and the strength to achieve it. Life is difficult and tough.

It's also unkind to many of us. So, the obstacles we have to overcome to succeed can be daunting. Many times, we aren't prepared for the obstacles. Are we ever prepared for bullying? Prepared for abusing drugs? Prepared for fear? Prepared for broken families? Prepared for shattered dreams? While we cannot fully prepare for the unknowns that may arise, we can certainly prepare ourselves to face them head on as they come along.

Sometimes, those obstacles come at us in the form of people. I once asked NBA superstar Vince Carter how he dealt with those kinds of obstacles:

> *Pavlina:* So, sometimes, in basketball or with regular stuff you do, people can say some really mean things. How do you handle it? Because, I'm in middle school and kids can also be really mean to me at times.

> *Vince Carter:* How do you handle it? I'm sure you've heard the term, "Turn the other cheek?" I think that's the biggest comeback you can give to a person who says mean things, as much as it might hurt you inside. I think the consequences, after having a verbal argument with them, sometimes ends up negative. You know, we see it in the news and people always are hurt in some way, because of an argument. It's the hardest thing to do and I'm not sitting here and saying I do it very

well. I think, when a person is mean to you and makes fun of you, or whatever, and you don't say anything back to them, it kind of bothers them. They're expecting you to have a verbal argument with them and they realize at the end of the day, they think, "Hey I can't get to them." Like a wall, if you can't crack the wall, you tend to leave it alone after a while.

Vince Carter: Everyone criticizes, critiques, what I do and it's frustrating. You're human, you're going to be frustrated, but at the same time, hold your head up high and be confident of who you are and what you've accomplished and what you want to accomplish, and I guarantee you'll go further than that person each and every time (from Pavlina Interviews Orlando Magic's Vince Carter).

Another interview I conducted with Matisyahu spoke to how our dedication to purpose can fuel us through obstacles, not so much by what he said, but by what he did. At the time of the interview, Matisyahu had long hair and a beard (it was before he cut it all off for a new look). He was also very public about being a devout Jew, so it was no surprise he had a lot of kosher foods on his tour bus. I'm not Jewish, so it was all very new and fascinating to see all these unusual things.

He was very family oriented and meticulously clean. I thought he was one of the nicest singers I have ever met, and his tour people were also great. I remember, towards the end of the interview, I asked him to sing a song, and he sang part of "One Day," which is a remix song that he did with Akon. I found out after the interview that he had a bad ear infection and had been resting his voice. But rather than tell me that, he went ahead and sang anyway. Singing and interviewing were part of his career. So, I imagine he didn't even think twice before he decided to start singing for me that day.

> *Pavlina:* Did you have any obstacles that you had to overcome?

> *Matisyahu:* Well, every day is an obstacle. Every day, there's obstacles, you know. Little things, just little things. I'm always just trying to stay centered, and focused, and thankful (from Pavlina interviews Matisyahu, who sings "One Day").

Now, for the majority of people I've interviewed, they spoke of their obstacles as opportunities to help them improve or learn. The problem with Millennials and Gen Zers is that we only see the obstacle as an obstacle. We have to learn that obstacles serve a higher purpose than simply causing us emotional distress!

If we don't handle obstacles properly, they can waste our time, set us off course from our goals, and potentially dominate our lives. Even the smallest obstacles, when approached improperly, can weaken our power, motivation, and self-esteem. That's not the life we were intended to live. I love how Sublime's Bud Gaugh put it when I asked him how he faces obstacles:

> **Pavlina:** Everyone I've talked to has had an obstacle they've had to overcome to succeed, whether they are a kid or an adult. Did you have any obstacles that you had to overcome and how did they help you get to where you are now?
>
> **Bud Gaugh:** Every day is a struggle. If you're not learning something every day, then you're doing something wrong. It's always a constant struggle to better yourself and do the right thing. As for me, it was alcohol and drugs. Those played a big part in my life and losing my best friend, Bradley (Nowell), to a heroin overdose really kind of woke me up. Now, I work really hard to maintain sobriety and keep myself out of situations that are bad for me. We have a zero-tolerance rule for the band and crew, and everything's working out great (from Sublime with Rome Bud Gaugh interview w/Pavlina).

As a twenty-something myself, I can speak to the things we fail at when it comes to facing obstacles. Thankfully, I can also provide ways to turn those fails into successes!

1. **We Allow Our Emotions to Rule**

    Typically, and I know I've been guilty of this, we tend to get emotional and then allow those emotions to take over a situation, rather than think things through more clearly. Drama is something we are famous for creating because it gets us attention. We love attention, whether it's good or bad. As long as it's attention, then we feel the power of it. Social media is proof of this! We post how we're having a bad day and friends immediately come out of the woodwork asking, "What's wrong?" and "How can I help?" It gets a reaction that makes us feel as though we have people who care, plus our post turns into a regular help column. That's not what we need to do. We don't "fix" our problem or obstacle by airing it to the public. The best thing to do is distance yourself from all the drama and social media when an obstacle arises so you'll have time to separate your emotions from the facts. Take a step back. Go to an exercise class, take a relaxing bath, or take a moment to regroup with a short getaway. Taking a moment to step back will give you a clearer sense of the problem and how to address it. It will help you approach the obstacle with a different perspective.

"Learning how to be still, to really be still and let life happen—that stillness becomes a radiance."
~ Morgan Freeman ~

2. **We Think, We Lack**

Resources such as time, money, network contacts, and experience are great. But I have found what's more important is the power of being resourceful. If you don't have the resources you need, then find a way to be resourceful. Everyone focuses on what they don't have, or what they want in the future, rather than how they can be resourceful right now to help get them where they want to go. As an example, I previously had an interview with folk singer and social activist Pete Seeger at Bryant Park in New York City. When I got to the interview, Pete's manager told me that since Pete is in his 90s and gets tired easily, I'd only be allowed to ask one question. I quickly did a mental tally and determined one question wouldn't be enough for what I wanted in my radio show. I thought about what I could do to change this. Ask more questions until I was pulled away? I had been given this quandary, with only a few moments to decide how I'd handle this once-in-a-lifetime experience. My solution? I asked my question and then I asked him to sing. Pete Seeger sang his song "Give Peace a Chance" to me. Later, he mentioned how he sang that song on stage before a huge group of people but couldn't remember who sang it with him. A quick Google search after our interview provided the answer—it was John Lennon. I took the obstacle I'd been presented and turned it into a memorable interview by utilizing the resources I had. By not focusing on what I didn't have, or couldn't do, I focused on a creatively original resource. That's the key to dealing with your obstacles!

3. **We Favor the Easy Button**

"We are kept from our goal, not by obstacles
but by a clear path to a lesser goal."
~ Robert Brault ~

Obstacles have a way of stopping us and confusing us about how to proceed. If we're not careful, we'll find ourselves all caught up in our obstacles, while our goals get more distant, because of our inability to sort through problems. If we take a step back and look at the problem from all the various points, then we have a better chance of properly analyzing things to come up with a solution. A bailout, quick fix, or instant solution is not an option! Different viewpoints and potential solutions can be added into the equation from friends and people you trust, but be careful not to seek their advice for a quick "get out of jail free" card. Overcoming obstacles will always require us to face them and determine the best solutions for ourselves. Our paths have constant sets of mountains to climb, rivers to forge, and challenges to face that are all essential to helping us enrich our lives.

4. **We Deny Their Existence**

We sometimes approach our obstacles like the monster in the closet. Maybe, if I simply deny its existence, it will just leave me alone. I know people who won't even admit to their obstacles. They've just lived with them for so long that there is no chance of them confronting those obstacles and achieving their goals. Instead, their daily rationalization is that they were okay with Plan B anyway, so that's how they chose to approach the problem. They disregarded the time they'd spent pursuing their original goal and settled for second best or just gave up completely. Rather than their obstacle being seen as a foe to conquer, it became a best friend that slowly sucked the life out of them. As Steve Forbes once told me off mic, "To succeed, you have to take risks. Make the point of taking the risk before your life turns into a series of plan B's." Don't become friends with the obstacle. Don't make up excuses as to why you can't deal with the obstacle. Acknowledge how it's been bumming on your couch, then kick it to the curb and overcome it!

5. **We Freak the Heck Out About Everything**

Even if we had all the money in the world, all the knowledge in the world, and all the resources in the world, we could not solve *ALL* the world's issues. Even so, for whatever reason, we personalize the world's problems and allow them to paralyze us much more and much faster than previous generations. We have to recognize how some obstacles are outside of our control. They will wipe us out, like a tsunami, if we allow them to do so. Instead, we should analyze which causes are most important to us and how much we can help with them. We'll have to learn to label these obstacles as "community effort" and then be okay with not being able to overcome them on our own.

6. **We Default to the "Right Way" Method**
Sometimes, we limit our ability to overcome, by limiting our attack methods. We see someone else face an obstacle a specific way and believe it might be the only way to overcome that particular obstacle. Maybe you have a student loan and the only way you know to pay it off is by working three jobs, as well as taking on all the additional hours you're offered. Be creative. Instead of asking for birthday gifts, ask for a student debt reduction birthday party! People enjoy helping others overcome their obstacles. Plus, they'd probably walk away feeling better knowing how much they really helped you instead of having given you a sweater you might not even keep. Regardless of your problem or obstacle, there is *ALWAYS* a solution. Sometimes, you just have to get creative in order to get it solved.

I remember one obstacle, in particular, I had to face and thought I'd have no option but to give up. I was spending the summer at Joffrey Ballet in New York City. I was thirteen or fourteen years old at the time. My leg had given out under a tough ballet session and I was wearing a leg brace. On top of that, my RA (resident assistant) wouldn't let me leave the dance dorms to attend an interview I had scheduled in Times Square at BB Kings. I had my camera gear together and was dressed and ready to go, but there was no way for me to get there. I called a relative, but they couldn't assist me. Finally, I asked a dance friend's mom to take me. Not only did she take me, but she helped me get backstage as well. I limped into BB Kings and did the interview, then limped back to my dorm. Naturally, the RA found out and gave me trouble about it for the remainder of the summer, but I dealt with it. Rules, I felt (and still feel), need to be broken sometimes in order to achieve certain things. I hadn't put myself at risk. I'd made sure I was safe by having an escort. The interview went well, so I was content and remained positive throughout the process. Not everyone would see it that way, but I found a solution to my problem.

During my second interview with Vanilla Ice, I was fifteen years old and asked how I could be cool like him (geez, I was such a geek). He replied:

Vanilla Ice: You just gotta be yourself, you gotta enjoy life, you gotta get out there and get in where you fit in and enjoy the experience. It doesn't matter what you have or where you are in life ... if you're happy you're successful it's simplifying everything. Get in where you fit in and enjoy the experience, it's all just a roller coaster (from Vanilla Ice Interview with Pavlina Talks Goes Amish & Ninja Turtles Orlando 2013).

> "I had many obstacles but not as many as some kids today. At first, I started off as a follower, I had to develop being a leader through trials and tribulations."
> ~ Shaquille O' Neal ~

Obstacles can be handled when you approach them rationally and with a clear picture of the problem. As young people who've gotten most things quickly, managing time with obstacles is probably the most difficult. It is so important to recognize some problems can be dealt with quickly. However, the majority of our obstacles will require us to curb our impatience and allow ourselves time to work through the problems.

CHAPTER 12

Determine What Motions to Go Through: Developing Habits for Success

After talking with more than 600 celebrities, traveling across the country for red carpets, and working with top people in their industries, you learn a thing or two about what they all have in common. Here are some tips I have learned along the way:

1. Wake Up Early

I have always been a morning person, probably because my mother made it known, from an early age, that if you were still in bed at 9 a.m., you'd wasted half the day. It might sound harsh, and I totally hated hearing it growing up, but she's right. Mornings are when you'll prep for your day and determine how productive you'll be.

In high school, I interned for the top radio station in Daytona Beach, *103.3 The VYBE*. I had to be at the station by 6 a.m. Therefore, I had to get up at 4 a.m. if I wanted to work-out, finish any last-minute homework, pack a lunch (for school that started at 7:30 a.m.) and be out the door in time to make it to the show.

I have always believed in the saying, *"The early bird gets the worm."* Mornings are quiet and peaceful, and it's the perfect time to get work done and help make your day less stressful. Now, my morning routine consists of waking up at 4 a.m., then meditating for 5-10 minutes. When I say "meditating" I mean going to my living room and listening to a podcast that helps guide me through daily meditation. It's not me sleeping for another 5-10 minutes and calling it meditation! This immediately puts my mind at ease and ready to attack whatever it is I'm doing that day. After my meditation, I get ready for the gym and do a HIIT (high-intensity interval training) workout for an hour. Getting your workout done in the morning is like making your bed. By the time it's 6 a.m., you've already done more than some people will do all day! Doing some form of physical activity in the morning gets your blood pumping and increases endorphins. This helps you start your day happier and with a sharper mind.

2. Taking Some Me Time – Especially for Sleep!

If you want to be successful, it takes an astounding amount of grit and sacrifice. But, to be effective, you also need to take time for yourself and recharge your batteries. You will make better connections in networking, and for yourself as well, when you're fully present. People can always sense when you're not fully present or engaged in a conversation. Lack of presence can be a major turn off!

I know I'm an ambivert, which is right in the middle of the introvert and extrovert scale. I love being around people, but I can get exhausted and need time alone to recharge.

It's important to carve out time in your daily schedule to make this happen, so that you'll maintain the best mindset possible.

A simple solution I love is just to take a bath! It's amazing how problems seem to melt away with a bath bomb and some candles! You need to figure out your Zen and make it a regular routine for recharging yourself. As for me, it's that luxury bath to help unload problems of the day and just zone out. I also take regular exercise—yoga, or meditation classes—that help me to release all the stress.

You can't enjoy your successes if you don't calm down and dial back the moments of each day. It's a matter of enjoying the journey. The amount of time that you're working hard and enjoying the experience is fun, but it's exhausting. You won't be able to keep up the pace if you don't step back once in a while and look at your vision. By taking the necessary time to relax, you're able to expand your vision, edit it a little, and regroup to push your strategy.

Everyone needs the drive to get ahead. Being comfortable in your position only lasts for so long, then the push is necessary to achieve your vision. The progress toward your goals may feel burdensome at times. You'll find yourself snapping at people around you and, quite honestly, anxiety will set in as well, which gets you off track. At the end of each day, these should bring a sense of progress when you reflect on it. The reflection you'll do while relaxing should have you going to bed giving yourself a high five with what you've accomplished and happy to embrace the next day with what remains to be done toward your goals.

This is a marathon, not a race—a life journey of accomplishments you've set for yourself. This needs to be a lifeline of good vibes. Each step may not be perfect, but it's something you are proud about and you'll enjoy the big and small steps along the way!

Get a good night's sleep! C'mon, we know this and, let's be honest, we're a bunch of mad and crazy people who don't appreciate the Zzzz's we need to thrive. There are parties, meet-ups with friends, and late-night studying that lasts too long. We find ourselves with sleep patterns that are permanently trashed.

I interviewed Ariana Huffington for her book, *Sleep Revolution.* She wrote that book after waking up in a pool of her own blood. She had been so tired from eighteen-hour work days during the two years she was building Huffington Post that she had fallen over in exhaustion and broke her cheekbone. After this, she began to dedicate her life and work to the importance of sleep.

I've had to work at understanding the greatness of sleep. I always thought that since I'm young I can easily bounce back the next day, but it doesn't happen. Instead, by noon the following day, I'm a wreck. I'm ready to slither into a corner from exhaustion and my work is not up to the normal standard I expect of myself, which gets me frustrated. It's hard to control your sense of wellbeing, when you're exhausted from lack of sleep.

Life can't be about grinding 24/7 or hustling 365 days a year. It's about going all in when you're working and hard-core resting when you take a break.

Your best work is going to happen when you take care of yourself. When you're well-rested, you are able to focus better on your task at hand. I know it sounds like, "Wow, Pavlina, if I'm so busy taking care of myself, working out, and sleeping, when am I supposed to be building my empire?" First of all, patience, young Padawan. Rome wasn't built in a day and it's definitely important to prioritize. If you wake up early and work-out, but then spend only half the day working and half the day with your friends—or watching Netflix on your couch—then your priorities aren't straight.

3. Focus on the Positive

We are known as the depressed, anxious, and lonely generation. It's not a great place to start, but valid as to the reason we've been labeled this way. In the age of social media and growing up fully immersed in the tech world, we hide behind the scenes and don't even know how to carry on a proper conversation. It's easy to compare ourselves to Kylie Jenner and want everything she has as well. Likewise, it can be discouraging when things don't work out for us. But, it has always fascinated me as to why we get stuck in these ruts and why we let it consume us so much that it literally makes us depressed. Did other generations face the same issues? Was it just not in their face as much as it is for us on a daily basis? I think the most crucial thing you can do is to develop habits for when you aren't focusing on the positive.

> **Vanilla Ice:** I call my followers the ninjas—they follow the same pattern I follow, which is positivity. Stay positive in life and karma will come back to you in a good positive way. That's why I always say smiles are contagious. The more you can smile the better you are" (from Vanilla Ice Interview with Pavlina Talks Goes Amish & Ninja Turtles Orlando 2013).

4. Patience, Young Grasshopper

The hardest thing for a twenty-something to do is ratio-nalize patience. We really see no need for it. We have in-stant information-gathering with Google, instant dates on dating sites or apps, and instant food with drive-ins or microwaves. It's an "I want it big" and "I want it now" mentality. Where does the need to slow down make any sense?

Unfortunately, big changes do not happen fast, but rather with a small, steady set of changes that can turn into a set of formed habits. Your life should be a life with signif-icance and it needs to be nurtured. Remember, this is a steady pace kind of race, not a sprint. If you just breathe through the hustle process, it will ultimately be more productive and filled with less anxiety.

Probably the biggest mistake I see twenty-somethings make is giving up. Their patience is non-existent. I re-member singer Andy Grammar talking to me about being an "instant" celebrity. He wasn't, really, not in his eyes. It took years of playing on the streets. Most people will tell you they spent many hours perfecting what you see as an "instant" greatness. The old expression that "it takes 10,000 hours to master something" is true! But what if you spent all that time, and more, working on your goals and it still hasn't gotten you to where you want to be?

Take a look at how you are trying to achieve your goal. It may take a simple tweak, or you may want to schedule a talk with one of your mentors and discuss the process. You may be right where you are supposed to be on the path, only you don't "see" your progress like someone else can see it.

Persistence and patience are the yin and yang of success. Persistence means you're able to push and be stubborn with what you want. I was called tenacious before I knew the definition of the word. I just knew I couldn't, and wouldn't, take "no" for an answer. If someone told me *no*, it became my personal mission to change it to a *maybe* or a *yes*. If they couldn't give me the answer, or results I wanted, then I'd approach someone who would do so. That wasn't showing impatience. It was just a matter of achieving what I wanted to achieve with the circumstances I was given. Many times, I was at a venue and I'd be told at the last minute an interview wasn't going to happen. Or, I'd have to wait for a bigger name magazine to do their interview first. I knew once the bigger media did their interview then my time would literally be down to only a few seconds, before the personality had to leave. This required me moving to a different decision-maker at the venue or performing some sort of "ninja work" in order for my time to count. I was patient when I felt it was worthwhile to be patient. And, I was persistent when I needed to be. This balance will bring you the most success, because there's no way you can only be patient and wait for things to happen. You need to know about patience. You need to know when to strike, too.

5. Planning and Goal Setting

Your vision board and goals are your GPS. There are roads to take that help get you to your next stage of the journey. And there are things you have to accomplish in order to reach your destination. What you plan to accomplish should be what you love. It's the satisfaction of the challenge that makes you happy and mentally strong. When you're building your success, your goals should be a path you enjoy. It can be frustrating at times, and there will be some failures along the way. But, you'll understand your reasons for doing what you're doing. In other words, you will understand "why" you are doing it, even if you don't always understand the "how" of it all!

Your planning shouldn't be about getting rich and all the great things money will do for you. It should be about doing what you enjoy and are naturally good at. I've never met anyone successful who just wanted to be rich. What I've found is how people do have the ability to find their purpose and something they are good at—possibly better than others—and the desire to strengthen themselves in their careers. Money and everything else followed this after they proved their strength in their particular field. Your talent makes all the difference in achieving your desired riches.

While you are working on your goals and taking those steps forward, there will be a day when, all of a sudden, people around you start asking for advice because they see you're achieving what they hope to achieve as well. I was amazed when it first happened to me. I started getting emails from high school friends or people I had connected with through a conference, and they were saying, "Hey, can you tell me how you did this or how did you go about doing that?"

Taking time out of your daily climb towards success to help those who are just starting their journey is a win-win situation. First, it helps the new kids on the block get some solid footing in their career journeys. Second, it gives you a moment of golden beauty to appreciate your hard work. Hey, someone out there has seen your climb and thinks it's pretty amazing! That's such a natural high! This dual role is great and helps you be a stronger person. Your goals do not seem so impossible when you're able to assist others who see you as a professional.

Planning your next move, and subsequent moves, should be fluid. Sometimes I talk to people and new ideas start running in different directions. That's both good and bad! Ask yourself if this new project or goal you're adding will be of assistance with where you want to go. Will the extra path add to your credibility? What do you gain from this? In my case, if it's media related then I try to make time for it and add it to my planning agenda. It may add a new goal as well. As an example, I regularly talk about issues, but when I was asked to highlight my media experience, I decided to embrace sharing my journey. By the time I'd done a few speaking engagements, my knowledge in different areas of media had advanced to not just being in front of the camera and mic, but behind the scenes in the producing aspect as well. Photography is another skill I added as well.

Your life will be more fulfilling if you're expanding your career into other areas that can enhance your field. Your talents should always increase, in my opinion, because it's a growth that will help to make you more complete, as well as being constantly challenged mentally. Plus, your value and worth will keep on growing as well.

I also want to take a moment and discuss keeping your goals realistic. While growing up, the kids I knew didn't set realistic goals. They would see someone famous and want to emulate them because they were rich and "had it all." I think that's where I had a bigger edge because I would have an overall goal and then smaller goals to help me achieve the bigger goal. I would also set a one-year plan and a five-year plan. Most importantly, I would accomplish a certain amount, but "fail" at some other things I wanted to achieve. Despite the shortcomings, I still kept plodding along with a mentality like water and rocks. The water can flow over the rocks, but the water can also go around the rocks. In other words, there are different ways to achieve what you ultimately want to achieve. The trick is finding the way to do it. You need to push yourself, but not to the point of getting frustrated. If your goal doesn't pan out, then reset yourself for another way to achieve it. Be realistic, be elastic and understand the process. Failure isn't failure, not really.

> "Failure is not the opposite of success.
> It is part of success."
> ~ Barry Popik ~

CHAPTER 13

There Are Only So Many Hours in the Day: Understanding Moderation

I spent my 20's really not stopping to smell the roses, going to events like this (Gracie Awards) and not living in the moment, because you get preoccupied with making your life a resume! CHECK! I need to have a job by this, I need to make this, I need to do this, I need to live in this, and you don't stop to smell the roses.

~ Tamron Hall ~
(from Gracie Awards 2015 NYC Tamron
Hall Interview with Pavlina)

Sigmund Freud offered the opinion that "love and work are the cornerstones of our humanness." This is important to understand because Millennials and Gen Zers have a tough time finding life balance. The foundation of what we need to build a meaningful life is difficult, because we struggle with the balance. Our human relationships are organized, for the most part, by our careers and work schedules. If we are able to balance our love and work, we're able to experience happiness. This all has a direct impact on our quality of life. Previous generations approached work like Fred Flintstone. Work was a way to provide for oneself and earn money. It provided a stable home for the family, vacations, nice cars and a house in the suburbs.

Millennials and Gen Zers don't want that American dream prize that is a byproduct of work. They want experiences, a top job to quickly turn into a passive income job, and money to make them financially secure. They don't want to tie all of it up into the "American Dream" their parents and grandparents deemed a successful life. Work needs to be a place of movement and a source of personal identity, as well as a place where we are making a difference. We want to feel a sense of self-worth and importance from our efforts. It gives us a footprint in the world and shows us a place in society. However, the love we have for what we do can make us one-dimensional. We are so focused with "eyes on the prize" that we don't take a look around and enjoy the simple pleasures. While it's great to be so focused, so driven, and so motivated that you live and breathe your goals, there comes a time when you need to step back a little and get back into the game of living. Explore your surroundings and take a day off. Cross out the calendar book of appointments and place a "me time" in red for one day. You need time to just "be."

I went through a burnout phase in high school because I was doing so much. Besides being in the International Baccalaureate (IB) Program (which was quite a rigorous academic program, requiring a lot of studying), I was also making trips around the state, either daily or three times a week for interviews. After conducting the interviews, I had to spend time editing them. It was constant school, work, and more work, with minimal sleep. The more interviews I had, the more it spun out of control. In addition, some venues also expected me to show up for media.

And, on top of all that, there was a lack of understanding with most of my teachers. The more lenient teachers were helpful, but even they felt if I was this busy in my career, I should consider homeschooling to help me stay on top of my academics. The time when I had to catch an early flight home from Las Vegas because a teacher wanted me to take an in-class exam was when the shit finally hit the fan.

It was at that moment when I decided to do my best but not break my back while aiming to please any more. If I was in Miami, then I'd study on the way home and not flip out if I got a C. Teachers didn't want excuses, so I wasn't going to give them any. Looking back, I could have been more diplomatic and communicative.

College wasn't much different. Being busy meant being successful, but stress followed as a byproduct of it all.

Of course, I'm not alone with this crazy, stress-filled pace. But when it came to deciding on a career, it suddenly became clear that working all hours and stress-filled days was not a career goal I had in mind. It also isn't a goal for other Millennials and Gen Zers, which is why we are changing the office rules. According to an article from Claire Can and Snam Yar of the New York Times, "...it's not about jumping up titles, but instead moving into better work environments..."[5] Boomers were all about the title and long work days and planning their lives around the job. Millennials and Gen Zers don't believe in this life sacrifice. The twenty-somethings are leaving jobs that are not empathetic with time management and corporations are seeing the shift; realizing if they want to keep outstanding young talent, they need to rewrite the policy.

Moderation and balance were not important to previous generations. Maybe that's why Gen Zers and Millennials are identified as lazy and entitled by the generations before them. However, these younger generations of today feel putting yourself first has more long-term advantages than being a slave to a job. More productivity is the result if you're happy at your place of employment. Your quality of life is abundant and those around you are relaxed. Your family life is more enjoyable as well. By redefining their workloads and priorities, Millennials and Gen Zers can then spend more time doing what they enjoy the most—having life experiences. That doesn't mean we are slackers in the workplace. It just confirms we don't subscribe to the obsession of the job and long hours at the office just to obtain a paycheck. Instead, we look at the byproduct of burnout, depression, and gender inequality, as well as never having time for children or our own personal endeavors. The sacrifice is too great and Millennials and Gen Zers won't pay the price.

Our sense of entrepreneurship is strong, so even when working for someone else, we push the envelope while demanding vacation/personal time and working remotely. We live in a digital age and being able to achieve the same amount of work from our homes as we would at the office pulls rank with many white-collar workers who would otherwise planted in the office. The rat race doesn't hold as much appeal to us as achieving a sense of independence by saving or investing in our own business, and becoming financially independent as soon as possible so we can spend more time with family and experiences.

We are very wary of the possibility of burnout. It requires more recovery time. It's also embarrassing to suffer burnout when everyone else around us is chugging along. Thanks to social media, everyone's life is filtered and fun. It's always a perfect day as you scroll through your friends' lives. But being a victim of burnout because you weren't balancing your life the way you wanted can be stressful in itself. How do you prevent it?

1. **Time**

   It's your biggest and best commodity. Take time to relax. We've grown up with instant gratification and instant results. Life is a series of fast and slow-moving results. There's a lot of preparation that's necessary to succeed with projects and goals. Groundwork takes time, and then suddenly things come together. Understanding this and being patient is necessary to help you in not getting over-stressed with your own time goals.

2. **Mentors**

   Mentors can help put things in perspective. They can also share about their own experiences so you don't feel alone in your journey.

3. **Put Down the Phone**

   Disconnect for an hour or more every day. Unfortunately, we need our phones for work. But, taking time away from it—an hour per day—can make a big difference with your mental stability.

4. **Focus on One Job at a Time**

   We are used to being on our phone, texting to someone else, and quickly sending an email to a colleague. This multitasking is stressful. You don't need to be a robot like this, so take a back seat for a moment.

5. **Don't Do All the Work Yourself**

   Delegate and get back-up people, a part-time assistant, or a personal assistant to help do the busy work for you. It will help you clear your head so you can do the important work, plus have extra free time.

Burnout with Millennials and Gen Zers is more serious than previous generations. We are already disconnected in many ways by being more individualistic in our lives. We've grown up in a utilitarian atmosphere and burnout can result in loss of a job.

Millennials suffering from burnout is at an all-time high. According a recent study, 84% of people surveyed say they have dealt with burnout, while at work, which is almost 10% more than previous generations.[6] It's also serious enough to make people leave their jobs. Nearly half of those surveyed in this study have left a job specifically because of burnout.

If you love what you do, then you have to ask yourself, "How can you suffer from burnout?" And if you are passionate about what you do, "Why do you need to balance what's so important to you in the first place?" It's tough to deal with this because it makes us wonder if we really love our jobs after all. This quandary has us taking a step back for a moment. If you love your job so much, how can there be such a sense of having an overwhelming work-load along with feelings of blandness. This happened to me and I started making excuses for myself. Maybe I was just sleep deprived or moody from a bad diet that week. Maybe I just wasn't focusing because I was losing interest in the work. I once read somewhere that one in five people suffer from burnout in their careers. Even though I knew about this statistic, I thought I was immune because I enjoyed what I did, and I was passionate about it and wanted to do well.

If you're experiencing exhaustion all the time, this can be your first red flag. This is a tough one for twenty-somethings because it seems like we're always tired. There's studying for exams, partying, meet-ups with people, and of course marathon Netflix sessions. Naturally we're tired.

The work no longer has your interest. It's a matter of not being engaged with the work you're doing any more. Additionally, there's a lack of motivation, with that blah feeling. Really, the spark is sort of gone.

I'm a firm believer that, if you are truly passionate about something, it doesn't just go away. The atmosphere you are in at the time may be toxic and result in burnout, or you may be trying too hard and need to take a step back for a minute. Give yourself permission to take a break and regenerate your thoughts as to why you first had the passion for this career and what has changed. Understand your limits and take a day off if you need to do so. Emails can wait until the morning. Don't become lazy and make that the norm, but don't kill yourself trying to get to the top either. Being uncomfortable with your passion is scary, but just step back for a moment and realize you can handle it.

If it continues, you can still take time off thanks to the *Family and Medical Leave Act.* Most businesses understand the need to get away and just regroup. The important thing to remember is there's always a way to deal with your situations.

According to the National Institute of Mental Health, an estimated 46.6 million adults in the U.S. struggle with mental illness, including anxiety disorders. While Millennials describe the biggest stress factors in their lives being money and work, Gen Zers also feel those are the main contributors to their stress. However, Gen Zers are more in touch with their mental health than older generations. And while Gen Zers talk openly about their mental issues, they are disturbed to find how many workplaces just sweep under the rug. Yet it appears to be an issue that refuses to go away. We're seeing more than half of Millennials leaving their jobs due to burnout. That is really staggering, but the number of Gen Zers leaving their jobs because of mental health reasons tops 75%![7]

This is becoming a bigger issue in the workplace today because Boomers rarely discuss mental issues and are certainly too embarrassed to raise the issue in their jobs. Millennials and Gen Zers, by contrast, have no shyness at all. They realize the importance of staying mentally healthy in today's society and all of the forces around them that make it so challenging.

Moderation and balance are both important in our lives. Work hard and play hard, but realize the balance is needed to keep you mentally healthy. A life that's out of balance with too much play will put you living in a van down by the river while a life overly skewed toward work could put you in a padded room.

CHAPTER 14

Adulting: The Money Edition

I've mentioned already how we stress about money more than previous generations. Millennials and Gen Zers feel as though they have way too much debt—and they do. It's a big circle effect because, for the most part, it's related to school debt. We go to school and take out loans, then the loans are bigger than we ever imagined because college is more expensive than we ever imagined! Suddenly, we have a ginormous college debt with, hopefully, at least a college degree to show for it. Many friends I know have college debt and they dropped out of school, meaning they have no college degree. God, what a mess. Others have their degree and massive debt from student loans, but no job in their future related to their degree because the degree basically sucks. That's a heavy burden for a twenty-something and extremely stressful. Besides having college debt, Millennials have other baggage on the donkey's back—credit card debt. According to a recent study, more than 53% of Millennials feel as though they have too much debt and are uncomfortable with their financial situation.

You would think most Millennials would set a goal to pay down, or better yet, pay off their debt once they get a regular job. That would lift a huge weight off their stress level, but sadly it typically doesn't happen. Why? Because Millennials need some financial education if they are to succeed.

I've suggested numerous times how school should include an adulting class. You know, a class that teaches kids the life skills they need to survive everyday life. Things like how to do your laundry, how to clean the bathroom and, I don't know, how to properly use money. But teachers and administrators alike shrugged it off or said it should be the parents who are responsible for explaining those things to their kids.

When it came to money, one of "those things" for me was not knowing how to write a check or balance a checkbook when I was nineteen years old. Not teaching kids these simple money skills is like turning your pet poodle loose in the forest and expecting him to survive. There's really no natural instinct on how to do this. Well, the poodle might have some survival instincts that kick in, but there is absolutely no money instinct that kicks in for kids. Believe me, I know! I could've asked someone to help me, like a banker, a co-worker, or a friend, but I was too embarrassed to do that.

So, with all that being said, let's dive into Pavlina's Crash Course in Adulting: The Money Edition. We've already touched on the first point:

1. Learn to Write a Check

This sounds like such a simple thing, but, seriously, do you know how to write a check? Maybe you think the world runs on credit and debit cards while checks are only something your grandma uses, so what's the need to learn this skill? Well, get over your high-tech self and learn to write a check! It won't take you very long at all and when you find yourself having to pay a bill by check, you won't feel stupid.

2. Keep Your Checkbook Balanced

The word "checkbook" throws us off, and I get it. It's simply to suggest keeping your account balanced. Again, this seems like such a weird thing to learn for those of us raised in the tech age. Honestly, that's why I have an app that shows me my bank account any time I want to see it, right? Having instant access to your bank account with online banking or banking apps is a great tool, but it doesn't 'account' for everything you've spent and that's the stuff people forget to tell you.

If you write a check, that deduction won't show up until the check is cashed. If you make an online purchase, or gas purchase, the actual amount may not show up for a few days. What does this tell you? It means you don't have as much money in your account as you do. It more accurately shows that when you think you have enough to make a $20 lipstick purchase, you really don't have enough, and then you'll get a nasty overdraft fee.

The good news is you don't have to use a paper checkbook ledger because like most things today, there's an app for it. There are checkbook and budget apps to help you record what you've spent or deposited into your account. This is helpful for a few things. It helps ensure everything is clearing your account, it helps prevent you from spending money you don't have to spend, and it helps keep you on top of identity theft. Weird charges are easier to spot when you know what you're spending and where.

3. Know Where Your Money is Going

A budget is important. There were times that I had no idea how much money I'd been spending on things. I swiped the card and wrote the check (once I figured that out) but had no clue what was really available for me to spend.

Controlling spending is a sensitive subject with us. We're adults and we consider all of our purchases wise and worthy. When I leave Sephora with a $100 purchase, I feel as though my money is well spent, especially when it comes with a free mascara with my bonus points!

Kevin O' Leary, one of the "sharks" on the TV reality show *Shark Tank*, recently made a comment in an article that cut deep into my heart and empty pockets. The topic was regarding my weakness—shoes!

> "You need flip flops, something to work out in, and two pairs of dress shoes—everything else, you're an idiot if you are buying more shoes. Because you'll never wear them, and they'll be sitting there for years."
> ~ Kevin O' Leary ~

Based on statistics, I'm not alone in my love of fashionable footwear. The stats show 75% of women in the U.S. own more than twenty pairs of shoes, compared to guys with an average of twelve pairs, and the average person buys about eight pairs of shoes per year. So, how does buying shoes have anything to do with budgeting?

Well, if you have any debt, and most people do, you'll recognize the real numbers. It doesn't seem like much at all when you spend $30 on a cute pair of shoes. But, when you spend $30 apiece on eight pairs of shoes over the course of a year, that is $240, which could have gone to paying off a small credit card versus adding to it!

When you begin budgeting, you'll start telling your money where to go instead of watching it slip through your fingers. It might not be fun to limit yourself from getting what you want when you want it, but budgeting will help ease the stress money problems can place on you.

4. Think Before You Purchase

A way of saving money and acquiring an intelligent way of spending is to think before you make that purchase. Impulse purchases are deadly. If you consider how much the purchase will cost in terms of how long you would have to work in order to make the purchase, sometimes that will freeze your hot desire to buy stuff!

An example is my $100 purchase from Sephora. If I thought about how many hours I'd have to work in order to get that $100 purchase, then maybe I wouldn't be as excited to buy it. So, for many twenty-somethings that $100 purchase is a whole day of working from 9 a.m. to 5 p.m. Is it really worth a blush, two lipsticks, a makeup remover and a free mascara? If I rationalize the items as necessary for work or a party I'm going to attend, can I honestly justify it? How much of that stuff do I already have in my makeup drawer?

Besides shoes, O'Leary said Millennials also waste their money on things like coffee (Help! Starbucks) and jeans.

So how does thinking, before we purchase, impact our money decision?

I said, "Help! Starbucks," because that was my life. I'd go to Starbucks and purchase the $5-$6 cup of coffee. What's $5 or $6 in my overall spending? It's no big deal and I could probably justify it. But, since I'm already there staring at that lovely pastry showcase, I found myself giving in to another purchase. And, that left me walking out of Starbucks with a few coins in change left over from a $20 bill.

That was my typical start to the morning and it adds up fast!

Getting up each morning and brewing my own coffee, which cost like twenty cents a cup, also gives me time. Instead of wasting time standing in the endless coffee line staring at the pastry showcase, I can make myself a healthy breakfast.

5. Own Your Money, Don't Let it Own You

A CNBC article published in 2019 stated that more than half (62%) of Millennials say they are living from paycheck to paycheck.[8] That's a daunting number. It shows our money is owning us much more than we are owning our money. So, how do we change that?

Well, back to my coffee experience. Saving $20 in the morning was instant and we love instant results.

That kind of instant result had me seeking out more ways to save. Since we are on the topic of food, I'll bring up another way I found myself saving money—meal prepping! I never felt it was feasible since I'm by myself, but my nutritionist told me it's cheaper and healthier. I respected her as the expert and went out to buy some Pyrex dishes. Each Sunday, I began preparing my food for the week ahead. I soon found this to be relaxing and really satisfying. I could make my own meals. I also felt confident I was eating healthier, thus losing a few pounds with the lack of sugary foods!

See how it can start with little things? All the little changes you make with how to spend your money will sort of snowball until you see, at the end of the month, how much you saved.

Younger Millennials and most Gen Zers are typically big spenders on specialty beauty and apparel products, and I'm totally guilty of that. In the past, I used the excuse that looking good was essential to my career. While that may be the case, I've found a few savvy shortcuts that help me save money.

My designer clothes have a short shelf life for me because they are used during a media event and then get re-sold at upscale consignment stores such as *realreal.com*. I make a good amount of money from reselling clothes and it's great for the environment because rather than getting dumped somewhere, the clothes are being reused by someone else. I edit my wardrobe every season, which used to be a costly endeavor. But now the money I make from selling clothes gets reinvested into new/vintage clothing that compliments my brand. By staying organized, there's less anxiety with what to wear or how to deal with the clothing. Everything is simplified, and I'm saving money!

6. Pay Off Debt

Gen Zers carry an average debt of $14,700. In fact, having a sizeable debt at a young age is the new normal, according to Chantal Bonneau, Wealth Management Advisor at Northwestern Mutual.

Debt feels like an albatross around our necks. Most of us feel guilty about our debt, which leads to more anxiety. So, we find ourselves having anxiety over spending, but still spend more because of our inability to manage money. It's an evil cycle that gets us, ultimately, more in debt, with more anxiety and depression over our inability to reach a successful answer to it all.

The answer is simple—pay off your debt! Easier said than done, right? But that doesn't mean it's impossible. Use your budget to see how much you really need for essentials (sorry, Netflix, we might have to shut you off for the next few months). Then, figure out how much more you'll need to help catapult yourself out of debt. Take on a second job or whatever other (legal) side gigs you can find. I know, somewhere along the way, you might be tempted to buy that new pair of shoes, but don't do it! Stay focused, hang in there, pay off that debt, and you'll find yourself with money to spend, no interest attached.

7. Respect the Benjamins

Insecurity with money probably hits most twenty-somethings because we didn't learn at an early age how to respect it. Yes, I said respect. My grandma knows how to respect money. The Great Depression taught my grandma the difference between necessities and frivolous items, and how to make the most of what she had, as well as being frugal if it was necessary, which was 99% of the time. So, by the time she was able to afford more, she still didn't disrespect the money. My grandma considered each and every purchase. You could count on one hand the number of luxury purchases she made during her life, but she had considerable savings at the end of her life.

Somehow, and I'm sure most Millennials and Gen Zers would agree, I think there should be a happy medium. I don't want to feel guilty for buying a luxury item once in a while. I don't think that is the way it's intended to be, but I do believe we need to respect the money we're making and think of obligations and necessities, and our futures.

We need to be more than the vapid generation society typically labels us as being. Our emotions should not be tied to our purchases. I know so many people (mostly females) who do emotional retail therapy shopping. They typically experience buyer's remorse afterwards, but that doesn't stop the cycle.

Respect the money you make. Recognize the time you spent to get that dollar and don't throw it away to the first person with a pretty product or catchy slogan.

"Experience is a painful teacher."
~ Steve Forbes ~

The lessons most of us receive on money come from older people telling us to learn from their mistakes. That's the worst kind of lesson because most people don't fully understand their mistakes. We look at them having to file bankruptcy and think, "Well, that's a bit drastic. I can't see myself having to do that." Guess what, they didn't see themselves having to do it either. It didn't happen overnight, it happened over time—one purchase here, another purchase there. Stuff adds up! Money is not a subject you want to find yourself failing at and repeating the failure over and over again. Learn from your mistakes or, better yet, the mistakes of others.

Take the lessons you've read about in this book and apply those to your finances. Set goals, make plans, and form habits to help set yourself up for success with your finances.

Chapter 15

Make It to the Top – That'll Shut Them Up!

Pavlina: What's, like, the best advice that you've ever gotten that you'd pass on to a young entrepreneur?

Barbara Corcoran: The best advice, ironically, I ever got was from my boyfriend/business partner, when I was 30 years old, and he'd left me and married my secretary. He said to me, "You'll never succeed without me." And, at the time, I thought it was the worst thing I'd ever heard in my life. But, you wanna know something, it got me through the next 10 years. Because, no matter what was going on at the time, I would think of those words and I'd just try one more thing to stay alive. So, I think an *INSULT* can, sometimes, sadly be the best motivation. And, for me, it certainly did the trick (from Barbara Corcoran Interview at ASI Orlando 2014 with Pavlina).

Have you ever found yourself with a dream balloon? It is shiny and new. You look at that balloon every day and feel happy and secure. Someday, everyone is going to love your dream balloon as much as you do.

Then one day, for no special reason, someone takes a nice sharp needle and pops the pretty dream balloon. It falls flat on the dirty sidewalk, where people step on it. Eventually it's swept into the garbage by the sanitation department. Even the rats didn't gnaw on it because it was worthless.

Sound like something you have experienced? You have a dream, but you're crushed to realize others don't respect and value it the way you do. This can hurt so much that you never want to pursue the dream, or any other dream, ever again. That pin rudely jabbed into your dream balloon didn't just take away the euphoric feeling of the dream, it also took away something else—your self-esteem, your worth—because oftentimes the dream defines what you love, what you feel successful at, and what you want to develop as part of your future. So, with your popped dream, your spirit feels less free. Instead, you feel trapped in uncertainty because someone has judged you as not being able to achieve what you put so much hope in achieving.

My crushed dream came from two people I trusted most at the time. I was ten years old and spent more time in the dance studio than anywhere else. I loved the studio, loved the classes, one after another, loved going to competitions, and loved the clothes. Honestly, I was at my happiest dancing. I was in the studio after a private lesson and usually we'd sit down and summarize how it went. One of the teachers told me what to work on for the next lesson and I nodded in agreement that I'd diligently practice and have the maneuver ready for my next lesson. Suddenly, the other dance teacher came over and yelled, "You can't sing, you can't dance, and you can't act."

I remember looking up at her and nodding, as her words crushed down on me. I didn't say anything. I wasn't even sure what to say.

However, I continued doing private lessons, continued receiving scholarships, and continued spending summers at dance camps in New York City. Despite her words, I continued winning dance competitions. But because of her words, I didn't really believe I was doing anything special. I'd discount the win as being an easy win because the competition wasn't fierce or it was because the judges liked my costume. It wasn't *me* who was actually a good dancer. I knew it wasn't me, because she had said so! I eventually left that studio. I found a less toxic, as well as more professional dance studio, where I'd continue my lessons.

However, a lot of damage was already done by that time and I didn't know how much until a lot later. At the time, I might have compared it to a slight fender bender. You think you're okay. You don't need any neck or back treatment, but a few years later you're suffering because of that "slight" injury. I suffered from that toxic, verbal whiplash, but it would be some time before I recognized where it all began and then found myself overcoming it to my satisfaction.

I talked with a probation officer once, and it amazed me when she confided that every time she went to the jail to interview an inmate, she was amazed she wasn't behind bars herself. That was an amazing statement to me because she was poised, financially successful, and was never on the wrong side of the law. Why would she think there's not much difference between herself and an inmate? Here was her answer:

"It just takes one thing—one little thing—and our world can change, possibly never to recover from it. The inmates come from all socioeconomic worlds. But, why did they go wrong and I didn't? The answer is that our makeup of who we happen to be determines this in many ways. How we fight to survive and struggle to take the next steps in our careers is crucial to who we are and become. Yes, there's some luck involved, such as the right time/right place thing. But your grit, no matter what life throws at you, is also a major factor."

The probation officer was right on point. The sheer nastiness of those dream-crushing comments could have left me bawling in a corner, ready to leave the dance studio and never return. Instead, my grit revealed itself. I wasn't going to buckle or back down. I was determined to keep my dream fully inflated, no matter how many patches I had to apply along the way!

How do you handle people who are dream crushers? And, more importantly, how do you persevere and carry onward after your dreams have been crushed?

1. **Face Reality**

   Admit that what they said felt awful, because it does feel bad. But then take a moment and look at yourself objectively, not how the dream crusher sees you, but how you know yourself to be. Don't buy into what they said or try to figure out why they said what they did. Analyze your potential and how you can get what you need in order to accomplish your goals. Their ugliness isn't you. Their words can't really affect your desire. Be like the Rocky Balboa movie character and toughen yourself up. Fight harder and stronger. Change the "can't" to "can" and the "you aren't" to the "you are." Dream crushers need to feel your success. Thanks to them, you toughened up and became a success. Every hardship, every difficult step in your journey, you were able to achieve because you wanted the objective. No matter what was said and no matter what happened, you continued onward to achieve success.

2. **Time**

   Prepare. Make a plan. Set yourself a time schedule—a month, six months, a year, two years, all the way up to ten years. Jim Carrey once wrote himself a check for $10 million dollars. He daydreamed during his struggling years and imagined himself earning that amount for his acting talents. He kept the check in his wallet, all those hungry years, as a constant reminder and incentive. This law of attraction can make a big difference in your goals. If you're always thinking about what you want and working towards it, then you'll attract it. Your time, preparation, and your will to believe in yourself can make it happen.

3. **Consider the Source a Minute Here**

   The bigger your dream or goal, the more likely it is that family and friends will try to "protect" you by stifling your dream or wanting you to shift it to be more realistic with what they consider to be a more common-sense goal. As an example, if your goal is to be an actress, your dad may say try it for a year, but still get that teaching certificate. Your dad has good intentions, but his statement is not very helpful. In fact, it can fill you with self-doubt because your dad thinks you won't succeed as an actress and wants you to have a career that can be more mainstream with a regular paycheck. You need to prepare yourself for the reactions of your family and friends, and be strong despite them. Outline your plan and objective so they can understand. They may not stand by you, but they'll know you're committed and will back off from discouraging you.

4. **Believe in Yourself**
Self-doubt can play havoc with you and slow you down from obtaining your goals. People around you can be jealous of what you're trying to achieve. If they think they can discourage you, then they won't hesitate to send a few self-doubts your way, bursting your dream balloon. This type of malice can be fairly obvious, but not always, and especially if it's a friend you've known for some time or even a family member. Distance yourself from them, or at least talk about their lives and not what you're doing—keep that private.

5. **Keep a Journal on What's Happening with Your Life**
This is great for your own meditation exercises, but extend the journal to your plans and how you propose to act on them. It's your timeline—the present and the future for you to reflect on and plan.

6. **White Noise**
Keep your dreams in that safe place for yourself, and when you're forced to hear any toxic comments about what you are doing, just treat it as white noise. Surround yourself in a protective force. Your positive forces can be stronger than their negative ones.

7. **Seek Mentors**

   Mentors can help shed some light on the obstacles
   and dark days you experience. But you also need to
   realize they can't do it all. You may need to depend on
   yourself, both financially and mentally, to carry onward through some of the process.

8. **Focus**

   Nothing worthwhile is going to be a piece of cake. It
   takes commitment and focus to get yourself to the
   end result. Also, sometimes other doors open you
   weren't expecting along the way. These can still lead
   you to the same goal, only it's a different course of
   action. Analyze these and be open to the possibilities.

Millennials and Gen Zers have an unlimited amount of
imagination compared to previous generations. We don't
do the status quo. We don't see a job as simply being 9
a.m. to 5 p.m., with a house in the suburbs. Doubters and
haters are the ones who can't see beyond a regular type
of life. Anything that is not ordinary must be wrong. Anything that is too much, must be too strange to be right.
Dreamers fall and get up. Doubters and haters don't
know what to do when they fall. They look to see what
others have done in the past. That is not twenty-somethings. The uncharted forest is an opportunity because
you aren't following someone's previous path. The forest
is scary because you don't have all the answers, but you
know you'll still pull through it. Being a dreamer has the

biggest rewards, along with the biggest risks. If you pursue your dreams, you'll come out stronger and be a leader from the process. You will be an inspiration to others who have similar dreams.

CHAPTER 16

Stop Looking for the Next Best Thing - Rock What You Got!

I was with a girlfriend one day and we were chatting about our work and our lives in general. She kept saying, "You're so lucky. I'd love to have a job like yours! You're so lucky to have it all." I stepped back mentally for a moment and looked at myself through her eyes. I suppose I did have a lot of things a girl could ask for or want, including a job that was not too demanding, for the most part, on my personal time. I also had a nice apartment, in a nice area of New York City, along with health club memberships that kept me balanced both physically and mentally. All of it was nice, but I didn't see it as being "lucky." I didn't wake up one morning and win some kind of life lottery!

It took almost ten years to reach this level of "luck." It took ten years of hard work and sacrifice. It took ten years of being a kid who thought like an adult instead of doing all the fun things kids do. And, honestly, I'm still pushing myself to that next level of success. Just like every successful person I know does as well. They keep on grinding. "Luck" had very little to do with it.

I should be flattered that it looked easy to be me. But I didn't want to bore my friend by explaining the amount of work it took for me to achieve a minor level of success. What was key to that "luck," or work, or whatever you want to call it, was the ability, early on, for me to brand who and what I was becoming. So, after a time, I became memorable when someone met me at an event or if I sent them a quick email.

This especially became evident with a travel host I emailed. He responded how he remembered me when I asked about having my show air on his network. I mentally did the math on when that could have been, and it had to have been more than seven years ago! That is memorable, not from a little luck, but a strategic branding effort on my part.

We have a huge misconception that in order to brand ourselves we need to be famous or have a product to brand. In reality, the most important branding is yourself. Some of the best advice I received on branding for my specific line of work was provided during an interview with DJ/ Record Producer/Songwriter/Radio Personality Clinton Sparks. And the funny thing is that we weren't even talking about branding.

Clinton Sparks: You meet somebody once you say, 'Hey how are you doing' and you might forget tomorrow. But, if you see me four days in a row in four different states, we're going to remember each other. I did that intentionally to build relationships with these artists. And, with most of them, I still have relationships to this day and we make music together.

Clinton Sparks: I kind of came up with a quote that I live by which is, "Be the first you and not the second somebody else." And, what I'm saying is most people try to do or be like somebody they already know or have seen. And, most people try to do what somebody else has already done. And, I've tried to make it a habit that if it feels like it's been done already, then I don't want to do it. Or, I want to do it differently, because obviously there's really no original idea in the world.

Clinton Sparks: Just being you is what's just cool (from Clinton Sparks interview with Pavlina Daytona Beach, FL 2012).

After that interview, I began attending conferences, meetings, and whatever other media-related events I could fit into my schedule. I wanted to meet people and see them again and again so I'd be remembered. This was part of my brand strategy. Key people began recognizing my name on the list. I found myself instantly being known when I walked into a room.

So, how, and why, do you brand for yourself?

1. **Be consistent**

   Ensure everything has the same vibe and logo, if you have one, across your website and all other social platforms. Make it easy for people searching and checking out your work to find the same recognizable "you" stamped onto each site.

2. **Win that First Impression**

   Realize that people make quick decisions, so make it easy on them. Have yourself already "packaged" with what they want and a spiel enforcing why they need you. Most of us, when faced with too many decisions, move on and don't make any decision at all or we go ahead and make substitution choices. If your brand is strong when a decision is in front of the people you wish to make a choice in your favor, then you will win! By having a strong "you" brand, or brand for your business, it helps people make their decision easier and simpler. If you are next to someone who does not have a strong brand, then that's in your favor too because having a strong brand increases the chance you will be the substitution choice. Remember being asked on a job application to "Name 3 words that describe yourself?" As an example, you describe yourself as a friendly, practical, big-picture person. So, if your name is Patricia, at a meeting you'll walk in and say, "Hey, I'm Practical Patricia, here to get this meeting down to the basics!" Or, you say, "Hey, you're talking to Big Picture Ben here and let's see the best way of handling this case." You get the idea. It's basically to distinguish yourself from your colleagues or whoever you want to label a brand with at the time, so that they can easily identify you as the go-to person.

3. **You're Judged, Whether You Like It or Not**

You have a brand, but what you'll do with it is up to you. What you show people and what you tell people about your successes, your obstacles, your beauty, your academics, and how you display all this for society is up to you. People all around make judgments about you every minute and every day, including your co-workers, your neighbors, and your former school friends. And they're making decisions about you that may or may not affect your career! Consider these as dots that form your face—Pointillism. Each dot is a person you are exposed to at some point or is exposed to you. The perspective of you is how they see you and make decisions relating to you. The impression you give to people also gives them the capacity to judge you and reach various decisions. They are making decisions on your brand, but not on your performance. You may not agree with this judging, but it's just the way society happens to be. Your brand, whether you have it professionally created or not, influences your career. So, you really have no choice in having a brand or not. It's more a question of asking yourself, "Do I want to build my brand?"

4. **Be an Individual**

When building a brand, you have to stand out. Build your brand based on your individualism. How do you want to differentiate yourself? What's your key contribution? Make it simple, concise, and clear based on how you want to be known. Your brand should showcase who you are on your best day. Make it accurate and be original. Keep it simple and make it a reflection of you. The great thing about this is that your brand describes your greatness and every day you carry this message forward.

5. **Be Authentic**

When you think of one name, whether it's products or people, it's simply because of the authenticity conveyed in the brand. Send out signals to signify your brand. As an example, when I started in radio, I had really long hair and always wore Doc Martens boots. Why? Because they were the total opposite of how you'd picture a radio host. I was young and funky and used that shock factor whenever I walked onto the red carpet for interviews or into a room full of executives. Like me or not, they always remembered me and remembered my name. These high-leverage signals are needed for you to make your statement. *You* decide what it will be. It can be something as simple as always adding something else after signing your name like, "Your go-to makeup girl," so people always remember you. It's simple, it's easy, and it defines you. That's the important thing.

6. **Keep it Simple**

Everyone has a brain that likes to keep things simple. It's called *cognitive fluency* and it's the ease with which information is processed. We like easy, breezy Cover Girl. We like simple and we remember it better. If it's complex, then make it simple. Make it easy on yourself. Simplicity in a brand makes it visually pleasing. And it's a great outline for how you do an elevator pitch to explain in just a few sentences what you do.

I spoke earlier of Gene Simmons' confidence. His confidence was evident when he talked to me about his branding during our interview. He's extremely proud of the hard work that KISS has put into their brand. Here's what he had to say about branding and KISS to me:

Pavlina: You've recently said in an interview that your faces are more well-known than the faces on Mount Rushmore. So, have you ever gone some place where people didn't recognize you?

Gene: No. Have you?

Pavlina: Ah, yeah, all the time. But like, you've never gone into, like, McDonald's or anything?

Gene: Well, by a lot of marketing appraisals, KISS are the four most recognized faces on the planet earth and I'll prove it to you! You ready? Okay, Sweden is a monarchy, which means they have a king and a queen. Do you know what the King and Queen of Sweden looks like?

Pavlina: No. Ha-ha.

Gene: That's interesting, because everyone in Sweden knows what KISS looks like. How 'bout that? You don't know what all the faces of Mount Rushmore are, but you know all the faces of KISS, don't you? Defense rests, your honor (from KISS Interview w/ Pavlina AFL Celebrity Gala- Orlando, FL 2013)!

LOL. Lesson learned. Don't mess with Gene Simmons. Branding is mandatory! Your brand may not be as big as KISS, but you have the potential to make it just as memorable. Realize you have a brand, and like a Tamagotchi baby it needs constant attention to keep it healthy.

CHAPTER 17

There Are Enough Haters in the World, Don't Be Your Own

I was at my favorite French restaurant in New York City one Sunday morning, with my usual Mimosa and açaí bowl. I realized as I went to pay I'd forgotten my debit card. So, I asked if they had Apple Pay and, thank goodness, they did. When I sat back down at the bar, another solo customer in his forties said to me, "I know this is a dumb question. I just got an iPhone and was wondering how you got your card to come up on your phone like that."

I looked at him, puzzled, wondering why he would think it was a dumb question and said, "No, it's not a dumb question at all, let me show you." I showed him, along with a few other tech tricks, then I took my to-go box with me and went about my day.

The day before that, I was at my yoga class and the receptionist was taking pictures. She'd asked if she could take a picture of me during class and I jokingly told her I looked like trash. I had just come from another workout, so my hair was still sweaty and I had it in a bun. And, I wasn't wearing any makeup.

She looked down at me and said, "Never say that about yourself."

At first, I was kind of taken aback by it, because I was only kidding, but she had made an incredible point.

Why do we put ourselves down like that? Why does our own self-esteem set ourselves up for others to see us as not worthy? It's a question that Millennials and Gen Zers really can't answer because they typically bash themselves, and others, all over social media.

My interview with Arun Gandhi (grandson of Mahatma Gandhi) sheds a little light on our feelings of self-esteem, as well as the negativity we seem to harbor:

> *Pavlina:* You grew up learning that non-violence is based on five elements: Love, respect, understanding, acceptance, and appreciation. Which one do you think is most difficult for people?

> *Arun Gandhi:* I think, in a sense, all of them are difficult, because we are so accustomed to being negative about people. We don't accept strangers very easily. We don't accept people of different cultures or color very easily. We have to learn to be one human family, instead of Americans and English and Indians and so on and so forth. We

are just all human beings (from Arun Gandhi Mahatma Gandhi grandson interview w/Pavlina).

Millennials and Gen Zers have taken that negativity a step further and compressed it into their own lives. The world is negative and we are negative. We have anxiety because the world has so much destruction we can't change (or feel we can't change), and to get a bird's eye view of it all we feel as though we have to be negative about ourselves.

Busy is how we define ourselves. Our work is organized, fitness time is rationed, and social times are included on our calendars. We are slaves to our cell phones because we don't want to miss a text or post. Everything we think we have power over, actually has power over us. Yes, we know this to a certain extent, but we are powerless to change it and our self-esteem crashes from all this powerlessness.

So, back to me not wanting a picture taken at the yoga studio because I'm sweaty and not looking my best.

"I look like trash." My friends say this all the time and we don't even think about it, because it's so common. The truth is that I had a spike of anxiety when the receptionist asked to take my picture, not because I'm vain, but because I had visions of it being posted on all the yoga studio's social media sites. Or, just as bad, I thought about a hardcopy of the workout picture being posted in the lobby. It only took a millisecond for me to visualize the worst about myself being judged negatively by negative people, when I really should have been fine with it. Honestly, how are people supposed to look after a hot yoga workout for God's sake?

How about the guy in the French restaurant who asked me for help with his new iPhone? "I know this is a dumb question, but..."

I immediately relayed to him that it wasn't a dumb question. You know why? Because, in that flash of a moment, I remembered being too shy in class to ask a question, thinking my question was dumb or was already covered and everyone else knew the answer except me. So, I would never ask my question. That same feeling came back again and bit me when I looked at this older gentleman, asking for my help with a tech question. He found it embarrassingly confusing, but I had spent my whole life going through Apple 4 to Apple 11max!

I became aware of it and recognized this feeling of having low self-esteem. That was the key to it—awareness—just as the yoga studio receptionist became aware of my low self-esteem.

Part of the characteristics of twenty-somethings is their self-deprecating humor. It's so accepted with us. It's also something we tell ourselves. But then, every once in a while, like when I was at the yoga studio or when I was helping the older gentleman with his iPhone, the self-deprecating humor really isn't funny and we should slam the brakes on it.

I've noticed on social media just how much we talk down to ourselves. At first, it was funny reading all the self-deprecating memes, but then I started to realize just how negative they happened to be. I laugh at myself all the time and consider myself a funny person with a good sense of humor. But after mindlessly reading and scrolling through these memes and self-deprecating captions, I realized they were actually bumming me out. It feels relatable and funny, until you really start to view yourself that way!

I started to think more about this. I think it's absolutely fascinating why we started doing this, why we continue to do it, and the long-term effects it will have on how we truly look at ourselves.

Many of us find self-deprecation comforting. Most of the time we are joking, sort of, but it's interesting to note how women do this more than men. This kind of humor we constantly dump onto ourselves seems funny, but it really isn't. It affects everything, including our self-confidence, our self-esteem, our productivity, and our well-being. Every study I've reviewed shows women use it more as a coping mechanism. And it can actually hurt the women who use it. Call it total discrimination, but guys typically roll with this better than women.

If a man shows confidence, he is often seen as a confident man. But if a woman shows confidence, she can sometimes be labeled as too dominant, too ambitious, or too aggressive. If a man is self-aware and voices his opinion, he is, once again, often seen as a confident man. However, if a woman is self-aware and voices her opinion, she is often seen as self-promoting or bitchy. Likewise, the same takes place with humor.

In a paper from the *Journal of Applied Psychology*, researchers at the University of Arizona and the University of Colorado at Boulder examined how being funny was viewed—male versus female. Women who utilized humor, the study showed, were found to be disruptive or distracting with their presentations, even dysfunctional. However, men who utilized humor in their presentations were received by the audience as useful or functional, even when it contained self-deprecating anecdotes.

This can be, and is, frustrating for women. I make no apologies for being a woman, but I know first-hand of jokes told by guys that are accepted as appropriate. However, if myself, or a female peer, pulls out the humor card, I'm often looked upon as not being a good leader, being unprofessional, or as the study stated, "dysfunctional."

Even self-deprecating humor, which can appear as more authentic, doesn't do you any favors.

Self-deprecation has become a way of life for us, as well as an accepted form of communication. It isn't until we pause and think a moment about what we're really saying about ourselves that we can see the overall problems, which can arise from negatively joking about ourselves. Could this be another layer of our negativity? Our anxiety with ourselves? How did this happen to us?

The biggest cause is our fear of failure. We don't want to fall short in the eyes of others, so we beat them to the punch, so to speak. If we administer the blow that says, "We're no good," and "We're fluffier than we should be," or wherever else we think we're falling short, this will save us from hearing it from someone else. We think we know what others are thinking based on the opinions we have of ourselves. Unfortunately, we're often our own worst critic and we never stop to realize others aren't laughing in agreement that we're no good, we're too fluffy, or we're falling short. Instead, they are laughing, because deep down, they can relate to the same self-depreciation.

How can you stop self-deprecation?

1. **Stop Apologizing**
   If you find yourself apologizing for no reason, it's a sure thing you're suffering from feelings of inadequa-

cy. There are no dumb questions. Well, maybe there are dumb questions sometimes. But the point is that you're not born already knowing everything. It's okay to admit you don't know something so you can learn about it from someone who does know.

2. **Stop Covering Low Self-Esteem with Humor**
   Stop feeding into social media memes that show self-deprecating humor as acceptable. I was on *tublr. com* and it was literally riddled with constant negative posts that were supposed to be funny. This post by Thelonious is bad, but wasn't the worst, by far. It was actually quite average, compared to most:

   "I genuinely look like a hobo and no amount of judging can change the fact that in order to actually make my hair look appealing I would have to cut about 30 minutes off the four hours of sleep I get or the comfort of sweatpants or the way my depression makes me stop caring about me. Stop trying. #genzhumor #genzculture, #genzquotes, #genzmemes, #studentmemes, #studentquotes, #selfdeprecatingmemes, #depression, #judgement.

3. **Stop Discrediting the Good**
   Start looking at the good you have done with your life. There are a lot of things you're really great at and you've discounted them as unimportant. They are really important and you need to recognize them as such.

4. **Stop Seeking Perfection**

   There is no such thing as perfect. Repeat that, because in our filtered society, we see things as needing to be perfect or it sucks. Perfection is an illusion. The most interesting people I have met are people who don't try to be perfect. They are unique and that's made them stand out. In many cases, they became very famous because of their uniqueness.

5. **Stop Depreciating Your Purpose**

   You have a purpose. Jokingly putting yourself down is not it. Understanding this and believing this will bring into perspective how you have a higher reason to excel. Some people experience this epiphany when they join a volunteer group and others accomplish this stronger sense of purpose and worthiness when they meditate. Whichever you choose, it can help clear your mind to help with understanding yourself better and releasing any trigger to help avoid undercutting yourself.

How we have come to communicate with ourselves and others is part of the problem we find ourselves facing now. Everyone has moments of doubt, but to accept all of the heavy negativity and self-deprecation we pile on ourselves can be troublesome in the long run and undeserving of your true self. Changing a little of your communication skills, as well as taking a more positive slant, can contribute to a more successful YOU.

CHAPTER 18

Mirror, Mirror on the Wall, I'm the Greatest One of All (maybe?)

"It's something I've really wrestled with. I've gone back and quizzed my parents. When I was younger, I just did it. I just acted. It was just there...it was just something I did...Now, when I receive recognition for my acting, I feel incredibly uncomfortable. I tend to turn it on myself. I feel like an imposter."
~ Emma Watson ~

"I have written eleven books, but each time I think, 'uh oh, they're going to find out now. I've run a game on everybody, and they're going to find me out.'"
~ Maya Angelou ~

"Sometimes I wake up in the morning before going off to a shoot, and I think, I can't do this. I'm a fraud."
~ Kate Winslet ~

The *Imposter Syndrome*, or *Imposter Phenomenon* as some call it, was first described by two Clinical Psychologists, Pauline Rose Clance and Suzanne Imes, back in 1978. They described it as a phenomenon in which people believe they are not worthy of success and they have a persistent belief in their lack of ability, skills, or competence, despite loads of evidence to the contrary. These psychologists found that successful people often externalize their accomplishments.

I'm amazed by the *Imposter Syndrome* for various reasons. First, on a number of occasions, any time I achieved anything, I externalized it and didn't know why. I never recognized my accomplishments as being extraordinary, even when people assured me they were magnificent achievements. I would always push the award as not being for me specifically because there were no serious competitors for it. I had achieved the award by default in my mind. One award would follow another and another, and I never recognized the pattern as a pattern of success. I'd say thank you, put the award on my shelf and focus on the next thing I wanted to achieve. Whether it was an award, an accomplishment, or a raise in my salary, it didn't really matter. I didn't celebrate the achievement or reflect on the success as being a true success.

Former First Lady Michelle Obama has stated she suffers from *Imposter Syndrome*, as do many other successful people. *Imposter Syndrome* can be a step toward depression if we don't cut off the non-worthy flow to ourselves.

It is one of the layers many feel we succumb to in our lives in order to achieve the impossible "perfection."

So, why do intelligent, competent, and highly motivated/successful people typically display this debilitating phenomenon? Nearly half (49%) of Millennials struggle with *Imposter Syndrome.*[9] The number of Gen Zers struggling with *Imposter Syndrome* is similar. But, keep in mind only the older Gen Zers have entered the job market, so their numbers will certainly grow.

Why does it especially hit Millennials and Gen Zers so strongly? Is it another layer of our anxiety? Is it part of how most of us had a childhood in which we were encouraged to be the best? Or is it because we grew up on social media, questioning if every post was fake or creating/filtering our own posts to achieve perfection? We grew up creating the fraud feeling. Feeling like a fraud in what we did, and anxiety-ridden over being found out is a source of anxiety in our minds. Any success achieved we feel is not deserving and we can explain it away. The belief we do not feel as intelligent and competent as we come across to others tanks our self-esteem. Plus, we feel that a highly successful female CEO is truly confident, compared to being fake. This circles back around to being alone in our syndrome, when in reality a high percentage of successful people have daily struggles with this phenomenon as well!

When I discussed this with Valerie Young, author of the award-winning book *The Secret Thoughts of Successful Women: Why Capable People Suffer from the Imposter Syndrome and How to Thrive in Spite of It,* these are some key points I took away:

> ***Dr. Valerie Young:*** For people who grew up or came of age professionally in the age of social media, there's two things happening. There's much more pressure on people. Because of social media, we can't all possibly be living our best life, but what we see constantly on social media is the upside of things. We don't see the challenge, the difficulty, the failures, so it's this "culture of comparison."

> ***Dr. Valerie Young:*** And, I also think, when you're raised by baby boomers, and certainly not all baby boomers, but I think a lot of us in my generation, middle or upper middle class, really pressured kids in a way that a lot of boomers didn't get pressured. To get into the best schools, to excel not only academically, but in sports, run for class president, be involved in the community. All so they could get into quite a good school.

> ***Dr. Valerie Young:*** Anybody who belongs to a group for whom there are stereotypes about com-

petence or intelligence is going to be more susceptible to imposter feelings.

Dr. Valerie Young: Certainly, if you're the first person to do something – the first woman, the first African American, the first Latino, the first person who's blind – there's that kind of pressure to represent your entire group. And, that's also true if there's not a lot of you. So, people of certain fields are also more susceptible. Particularly in the STEM fields.

Dr. Valerie Young: I think if there was a core reason...Nobody likes to fail or make a mistake or have an off day or not know the answer or fluff some words in a talk or in a podcast, but when any of these things happen with those of us with Imposter feelings, we experience shame. And, the reason we feel shame is we have this unrealistic, unsustainable expectation for ourselves for what it means to be competent. So, what everybody wants is to stop "feeling" like an imposter. But, that's not how it works. Feelings are the last to change. You know, people who don't think like imposters, they're no more intelligent, or capable, or qualified. They just think different thoughts. In the exact same situations – in a job interview, or making a presentation, or being questioned on your work in a meeting – where we might have this imposter trigger, they're responding differently, because they're thinking different thoughts. This is good news, because it means all we have to do is learn to be like non-imposters (from *If God Had a Podcast* "S2 EP2: What Makes You an Imposter? Dr. Valerie Young Explains Imposter Syndrome).

How do we get away from feeling like an imposter and start thinking differently?

1. **Start Thinking like Non-Imposters**
   To break free from Imposter Syndrome, you must adjust your thoughts on what is necessary to be competent. Therefore, to be a non-imposter, you'll need to have a new outlook on how you view things, such as failures and mistakes. You'll also need to evaluate how you handle criticism and fear.

2. **Accept the Uncomfortable**
   Imposters feel they should be confident twenty-four hours a day, every day. Non-imposters know that they, and everyone else around them, have moments of fear, self-doubt, and lacking confidence. Rather than viewing these things as malfunctions, like the imposters do, the non-imposters will view them as simply being human. They will label these malfunctions as minor obstacles and overcome them, one step at a time.

3. **Don't Be a Pig, Be a Duck**

   Ducks go into the water and float. Their feathers provide a coating that helps keep the water gliding off rather than penetrating to their core. Pigs just swallow up anything set in front of them. Millennials and Gen Zers, as a whole, are not very good ducks. We swallow up whatever criticism is served! And, to all my female readers, you know we are even worse. Think duck! Criticism is all around us, and we need to learn to let it slide off us, rather than gobble it up.

4. **Seek Improvement, Not Perfection**

   Imposters seek perfection. Since perfection is unattainable, this search leaves them feeling empty, all the time. Non-imposters accept that perfection cannot be obtained. Instead, they seek improvement. They request constructive criticism so they can improve themselves and learn to work more efficiently. Likewise, they don't find themselves feeling shame because they didn't get a promotion or made a mistake during a speech. They move along with a "there's always next time" kind of attitude.

5. **Be Okay Without All the Answers**

   Imposters often find themselves feeling inadequate because of their lack of knowledge. Who wants to live with that kind of pressure? Even the smartest person doesn't know everything! Non-imposters have more of a realistic attitude when it comes to knowledge.

They accept the fact that they don't need to, and won't ever, know everything. There are things they will have to take time to figure out and there are things they will have to seek help from others to accomplish, which leads nicely into my last point...

6. **Utilize Your 'Phone a Friend'**
    Imposters typically live on the island of "I." However, non-imposters live in the community of "We." Remember the game show *"Who Wants to Be a Millionaire?"* The contestants didn't have to know everything, they had other options that could be utilized to help get them through the game. The *50/50* option narrowed the answers down to two choices, *Ask the Audience* took a poll of the audience's guess at the answer, and *Phone a Friend* allowed them to call someone they thought might be able to answer the question. The contestants didn't have to be smart, but they did have to understand how to successfully get assistance. Have a pack of go-to people near you who can assist if and when you need them.

Men are generally more confident and comfortable walking into a situation or job and just sort of figuring it out as they go along. Who needs things like instructions or directions? Just wing it! However, women are typically wound up much tighter on the details. Why would you even think about putting something together without instructions or going somewhere without GPS? That's absurd. Even in these typical stereotypes, we can see *Imposter Syndrome* at its finest. Men have been seen throughout history as the ones who blazed trails in exploration. It's no wonder why they experience confidence in choosing a destination and getting there. By contrast, the women portrayed to us for so many years were often simple and quiet and were best at keeping homes.

The Millennials and Gen Zers are breaking through stereotypes like nobody's business and no other generation before them. Women are standing up and seeking equality in the workplace. At the same time, men are requesting things like paternity time to help show the value they place on their families. It's no wonder that, in turn, they are suffering from *Imposter Syndrome* as well. It's really only natural to feel some fear when you are pushed outside of your comfort zone. Everyone experiences some fear.

The issue is that imposters misinterpret the fear. Imposters believe that because they are not feeling great about their accomplishments, then they must frauds. They may also think, since there's no clear direction on the new trail they're blazing, they really can't do the task and they'll be caught in the lie soon. They also believe the confident people around them don't feel insecure or fake. Finally, they think it's just them feeling like this. The don't realize how most people feel the same discomfort at one time or another!

Pavlina: Why are people talking about this *Imposter Syndrome* so much now? I feel like we've heard a little about it the past couple years. But, I feel like, recently, it's really been in the forefront.

Dr. Jessamy Hibberd: I think, in part, it's an acknowledgement that this is a really normal feeling. When I told people that I was writing the book, *The Imposter Cure*, somebody's comment to me was, "I've got that! Do you think it's normal?" But, before that, I think, it was almost like it was embarrassing, or shameful, to admit having those kinds of feelings. Whereas, it's much more out in the public now and people are starting to realize that this thing has a name.

Dr. Jessamy Hibberd: The other thing is that we're getting more and more into trying to do everything perfectly, so when we're feeling that we're not doing well enough or that we're falling short—sometimes we believe it. It says something about us. That we're not good enough or that other people are getting it right and we're not doing as well. Instead of seeing that's just part of being human, and we really only hear what's going on in our heads. But, we judge that against what we see of everybody else's outside. So, we are doing this unfair comparison and imagining that everyone else has it all together, but you forget we can't hear what's going on in their heads (from *If God Had a Podcast* S2 EP4: The Imposter Syndrome and its Cure with Dr. Jessamy Hibberd).

That's a profound statement by Dr. Hibberd that I think deserves repeating, "We forget we can't hear what's going on in their heads." People really don't have themselves all together, as much as we think they do!

The *Imposter Syndrome* can happen in any walk of life. It doesn't matter your age, race, or gender. It's important to recognize it is a real thing and real threat so we can free ourselves from its suffocating weight.

CHAPTER 19

Start Making Your Money Work for You

"I used to say why save money if I'll die
tomorrow, I haven't died yet and I
have nothing to survive on."
~ Bangambiki Habyarimana ~
The Great Pearl of Wisdom

"How you do money is how you do life."
~ Orna Ross ~

"If I could sum up, when asked about
money in one sentence, how I feel, I'd
say "insecure. I feel insecure."
~ Pavlina Osta ~

In Chapter 14, we went through *"Pavlina's Crash Course in Adulting: The Money Edition,"* so you might be wondering why we're talking about money again. Well, let's look at this as Version 2.0. In Chapter 14 we discussed the basics every twenty-something should know about money, including how to balance a checkbook, write a check, get out of debt, etc. In this chapter, I want to dive into it a little bit deeper to reinforce some of the things we talked about in Chapter 14.

Charles Schwab's 2019 Modern Wealth Report showed Millennials to be the most insecure of any generation with their finances. Most Millennials say they live paycheck to paycheck. However, just as disturbing are the irrational/ spontaneous purchases that suck their paychecks dry. Overspending on non-essentials and luxury items is all part of the "I want it now" culture, and let's just say it ... feeling entitled. You get it, right when you want it.

This makes for horrible money management. And I'll be honest here that money management is more of a dark mystery to me. It's frightening, intimidating, and some-times hopeless. I want to save money, but there's always this daunting feeling that I am not saving enough of it or that I'm not doing it correctly (funny how this is follow-ing the Imposter chapter). So, with all the advice avail-able out there, what is the best route to take? Just like every other piece of advice in this book, there is no magic formula that works for everyone.

Some people like the traditional savings account route and others choose to invest their savings in stocks. Some people like to aggressively attack debt and others choose to pay the minimum amount due every month.

Saving money can feel painful, but it doesn't have to be. Yes, it's a sacrifice we are all too often unwilling to make, but we can change our mindset to help us reach our goals. If we aren't saving money, there's a good chance we're going into debt to make our purchases. If we haven't saved money to purchase that new outfit, there's a good chance we're going to charge it to a credit card.

Debt is a heavy stress load to carry and it can ruin your day-to-day life, your future prospects in love and marriage, and your future in business. In fact, it's the strongest anxiety burden Millennials carry with them today! It's always looming over your head and it doesn't go away. Every time you spend money, you'll find yourself feeling guilty or having buyer's remorse. You already owe whatever amount, so was it a good choice to borrow more? It's an awful, awful feeling. It's terrifying, the amount of damage debt can do to you and I'm not talking about your credit score here.

> "Why anyone chooses to live a life in debt
> has always been a puzzle to me."
> ~ Oprah Winfrey ~

Okay, I get it, that's coming from Oprah and you're thinking, "Well, yeah, but she has how much money and I'm sitting here making minimum wage." But Oprah wasn't always in such a great position! If you really want to have a breakthrough in your finances and the way you view them, you'll have to look at things differently.

1. Wants vs. Needs

Back in Kindergarten they had this exercise where we would cut out little squares with pictures on them and glue them to paper. One half of the paper was for *needs* and the other half of the paper was for *wants*. Where does the doll go? *Wants*. Where does the food go? *Needs*.

Let's try the Gen Zer version of this exercise. Where does the Starbucks go? *Wants*. Where does the make your coffee at home go? *Needs*. Seriously, let's be real. Very few of us can cut it out altogether, right? Where does the pair of shoes required for work go? *Needs*. Where does the $200 designer shoes go? *Wants*.

Do you see where I am going with this? In order to stop the anxiety over finances, we must return to some simple lessons to help keep us grounded. Bust out your college-ruled paper if you must, and jot down the things you're thinking about buying. Toilet paper is a necessity. But a bottle of vodka? Well, it depends on the...just kidding, you get the point.

2. Keeping Up with the Joneses, or for Our Generation, the Kardashians

There's a lot of talk nowadays about minimalizing. People are moving into tiny homes, cutting back on their wardrobes, and eliminating the clutter. I don't know if I'm on board with all of that because I feel like my apartment is already tiny enough. But let's take all that and ask, "What say you?"

Back in the day, they called it "Keeping up with the Joneses." The neighbor gets a new car, so you get a new car. Your favorite celebrity takes a trip to Hawaii, so you take a trip.

Essentially, it's a vicious financial game of follow the leader that ultimately leaves you as the loser, because with every purchase you make to compete, you lose a little of yourself.

Don't try to keep up with anybody else when it comes to purchases. Purchase with purpose! Does the item fit your brand? Be you, don't copy someone else. Does the purchase fit your life? That home gym sounds amazing, but why waste your money when you're an extrovert that enjoys heading to the gym each day? Be true to who you are with your purchases.

We are bombarded every day via social media and commercials telling us how we should spend our money. Friends purchase new furniture for their apartment and suddenly our couch seems old and dull, even though it's only a year old. Apply your self-awareness to your purchase as well. Stay away from "keeping up" with anybody else through your purchases.

3. The Greener Grass

This is another take on keeping up based in thinking the grass is greener somewhere else. So, maybe you accept the fact that your friend bought a new convertible and that's not really your thing. You can't help but feel a little jealous they have the latest model while you're driving the same car from high school, which you have to enter through the passenger door, because the driver's door won't open.

There's a YouTube video with a little girl trying to buckle herself into a car seat that says it best, "Worry about yourself!"

You've no idea how long your friend had to save money for the purchase or what kind of debt they have now that they're driving a shiny new car. Wishing you also had what others possess is counterproductive to your own finances. The better route to take is goal-setting. If you'd like to have a new vehicle in your future, set goals to get there instead of wishing for it, or worse yet, making a purchase you really can't afford!

4. Define "Emergency"

A really great goal is to ensure you have an emergency fund. This is money you've set aside somewhere that you're not allowed to touch unless it's an emergency. A lot of financial advisors recommend having $1,000 in an emergency fund. So, what constitutes an emergency? The TV you've been eyeing for a few months now goes on sale for $400 less than the original price? Not an emergency. Your favorite athlete releases a new line of shoes and there's only going to be 100 pairs of them on the market? Still not an emergency. You trip as you're crossing the street and find yourself in the hospital with a $200 bill? Emergency! Someone knocks your phone from your hand and the screen shatters so you can no longer use it? Well, first of all why are you attempting to look at your phone while you're walking? But, yes, we'll label that $80 screen repair as an emergency, because you do all your business via your phone.

Get your emergency fund built up and ensure you have clearly defined what constitutes an actual emergency for yourself.

5. Three to Six Months of Expenses

Aside from the "emergency" fund of $1,000, another form of emergency fund is to ensure you have three to six months of expenses set aside in savings. This requires figuring out how much you spend on all your essential bills each month and setting aside enough in savings to cover several months of those expenses.

This helps to relieve the "what if" anxieties. You know what I'm talking about, the "what if I lose my job" or "what if I get hurt and can't work" kind of anxieties. Again, don't get caught up on what you don't have at a particular time, and don't look at it as a monstrous amount to set aside. Instead, set small goals and work to get there. Having this money in savings will help to give you some security and breathing room. It might require some sacrifices to get there. You may have to put your tax refund into savings instead of buying that new TV. You may need to pick up a second job for the next year. Whatever it is for you, set your goal and make it happen.

6. College Fund vs. College Debt

Maybe your parents paid for your college or you had a free ride on scholarships. Maybe you never went to college because you didn't have the money to do so, but you're now wishing you did. Hey, you're still alive, so there's still time. Save some money and look into all your options before just accepting that "everyone has a college loan." That's totally fake news!

I'm one of the fortunate few with no college debt, mostly because I applied for every scholarship I could and worked my butt off to avoid college debt.

I'd sell back my books at the end of each semester or borrow someone else's books. It wasn't a major expense like tuition, but books add up. If I could get by without buying them and instead borrow someone else's on weekends, that's what I'd do.

I also went to the school that gave me the most scholarships. A full ride, or almost a full ride, is a huge advantage in my book, and it really didn't matter whether it was a top school or not. I had enough confidence in myself knowing it wasn't the school that would get me the job. *I* would get the job after graduating based on *me*.

7. GET OUT OF DEBT

Seriously, we are going to talk about this again. Even though Millennials and Gen Zers have more debt than previous generations, it's not a doom-and-gloom time for us. We've got what most do not have on our side, and that's health and time. Debt is not something you need to accept as the norm. Merriam-Webster.com defines "debt" as *"A state of being under obligation to pay or repay someone or something in return for something received: a state of owing."* I don't know about you, but I don't like owing anybody anything.

If you have any kind of debt, whether it's a student loan, credit cards, or car loan, pay it off. Develop a plan to get rid of it. Some experts suggest paying off the smaller loans first and once they are eliminated, then take that amount and apply it to another debt. Eventually, you'll be completely debt free and it will be an amazing feeling.

It's important not to be content with debt, but be focused on eliminating it.

8. Knowledge is Power

Pavlina: As a young entrepreneur, if I started out with $1,000, where should I put it?

Barbara Corcoran: I will tell you where not to spend it—on a patent. Everybody does. Giving the attorney money to do the patent, so you are helping his business instead of your own. I think the only thing you should be spending money on is anything that directly leads to sales. It's the most overlooked simple truth in building every business in America. If you're not gonna sell something, you're not going to succeed in business.

Pavlina: What should young business people, like me...how should they find their business partners?

Barbara Corcoran: It's essential that you use your own money, as best you can, to get started. I really think that kids too easily ask for their parent's money, "hey you want to believe in this". There are so many lessons to be learned, when you are burning through your own money (from Barbara Corcoran Interview at ASI Orlando 2014 with Pavlina).

Media is my area of expertise, not money. So, when I want to get some knowledge about how best to manage my finances, I seek out those who are doing it best. This can be a hard thing to do, because a lot of people in America are pretty private about their finances. If you happen to find someone who is knowledgeable about saving, investing, or getting out of debt, absorb what they have to say. Take their words and use them to form a plan and get ahead.

Don't allow people to talk you out of your money. Spend it where you want to spend it. Don't put yourself in debt to anyone, including your parents, loans, credit cards, etc. Regardless of how you choose to spend, save, or invest your money, I hope you take away this one lesson: Do it with purpose.

CHAPTER 20

Reaching Your Potential

"And let us not grow weary while doing
good, for in due season we shall reap if
we do not lose heart."
~ Galatians 6:9 ~

Reaching your full potential is a journey. It's an ever-changing, elastic, and fluid journey during which you adapt and grow along the way. The destination doesn't define success, it's the process and journey. I think we get lost with what we really want to achieve in life and what we think we should want and achieve because of society's norms. Your map is your own unique blueprint and shouldn't be duplicated, except in the basic steps to succeed, and even those can be freeform. I've learned, with anything I have ever undertaken, to be consistent with the routine and that's what leads to successfully achieving your goals. Your life of self-fulfillment, as well as successes in society that are important to you, requires time and motivation—and a plan. Understand the need to overcome obstacles, regardless of how difficult they happen to be. Sometimes you might feel alone when facing these obstacles. But there's a power within yourself, and all around you, that will help you overcome and conquer those obstacles—belief in yourself.

Your courage plays an immense part in achieving a better life for yourself. It also sets the stage for taking on the obstacles you have to overcome.

Every generation might feel as though they've had obstacles no one understands or has had to deal with before. However, the newest generations have a greater climb than others for a variety of reasons. Our "instant gratification" mindset has to be reprogrammed thanks to the technical revolution we were born into. We have problems that necessitate small steps to correct and time to deal with accordingly, which is a challenge for those of us who have obtained so many life moments instantaneously.

We need to be evaluate our lives and edit them on a regular basis. If we ignore problems, they can suddenly become too large for us to handle, which is when anxiety kicks in. Small steps can turn into a large leap when we stay serious about our commitment. That commitment should be in all aspects of our life—our jobs/careers, our family, our health, and our relationships.

I've seen people who couldn't reach their full potential as a person because of anxiety. Society is not kind. Our main goal—our ultimate goal—should be reaching a potential where we have a strong sense of life and love. The tools we've learned to use help lead us to a more fulfilling life that not only benefits us, but also transforms us into better people who can then help others improve and make society better. Some might say that person's a leader, some might say that's a spiritual person, and others might say that's a person who is mighty and tough. It's important for you to be real. It's important to be a better you for a better us.

That being said, to reach your full potential you'll have to implement the first nineteen things I said you'd need to know. So, let's review:

1. Age is Not Your Excuse, It's Your Advantage!

You should never, ever, utilize your age as an excuse. "But, Pavlina, I cannot become a fitness coach at ten years old." Excuse! You may not be able to obtain a license to practice, but that shouldn't stop you from practicing. Learn everything you can along the way. This applies to all kinds of stuff. My first interviews felt clunky and awkward. Oftentimes, people looked at me like I was joking when I told them I was there to conduct an interview, but that didn't stop me. I was determined to get better with every interview I conducted.

2. Refocus from the Negative

Negativity will drain the life out of you, quite literally. Learn to distinguish between flat-out negative words and constructive criticism. Having someone say, "You didn't do very well" shouldn't destroy you to the core. Do you want to learn how to properly deal with negativity? Get down on the ground and do five push-ups. Just five. Guess what? If you're not someone who works out, those five push-ups are going to seem impossible! But if you do five push-ups every day for five days, you're going to realize it gets easier and you'll be less resistant. Receiving negative feedback is never easy. However, if you filter it through the lens of constructive criticism, it will get easier. You'll begin to decipher what is useless crap and what can be used to help you improve.

3. You've Got a Dream? Awesome – Now Make It Happen!

Where do you want to go and what do you want to do? Okay, that's great! Now get out there and go do it! Make the commitment to achieve what you want to do. Maybe you don't have all the details worked out on how it is going to happen for you, but you'll have to start working toward it.

4. Face It, You're Gonna Fail

Nobody wants to fail, or think about failing, ever! We want to focus on success. We want to live in this fantasy world where everything goes exactly as we plan it, but we all know that never happens. Success is great, but failure can be even better. Failure builds up strength and resilience that isn't found with success. Look back at times when you failed. Instead of melting into a puddle of despair, think about how you can improve to help prevent failure. If you did everything humanly possible to the best of your ability, then accept that instead of beating yourself up. Accept that there will be things out of your control and move onward.

5. Stop Searching for Answers and Start Moving

As the saying goes, "Keep Calm and Carry On." If you have an idea as to what you should do, stop trying to affirm it by searching twenty other outlets. At some point, you'll have to stop questioning, stop researching, and start moving.

6. You'll Never Be Happier Than When You Learn to Love Yourself

Take time to appreciate yourself. Take time to appreciate what sets you apart from others. I'm not telling you to stand in front of the mirror and point out all of your 'flaws'. I'm telling you to stand in front of the mirror and appreciate every part of you. There is only one you. Love yourself. Secondly, take time to be happy. Life is busy and 'go-go-go-go-go' most of the time. Stop. Breathe. Laugh. Appreciate the simple things that made you smile as a kid. That small flower, fighting through the crack in the sidewalk. The beautiful colors splashed across the sky during a sunset. Or, the rain streaming down and forming puddles below your window. Find happiness.

7. Think You Can't, and You Won't, Think You Can, and You Will!

Henry Ford put it this way: "Whether you think you can or whether you think you can't, you're right." One will never recognize, let alone reach, their potential without the right mindset. Mindset is certainly a driving force in all of it. Where you see yourself going is where you'll eventually end up.

8. Plan to Do It and Get It Done

You are the only you. So, what's the point in doubting how you do something? Go into the world and do things to the best of your ability. When that doesn't seem like enough then believe that you can learn to do it a better way. Giving up on yourself is not an option.

9. Be Brave

Remember *Courage the Cowardly Dog*. Courage is not about being a hero all the time. Instead, it is more about standing up for those you care about and standing up for what you believe is right. If you fail to do this once, don't discredit yourself as a coward. Instead, dig down a little deeper and develop the grit it takes to stand by what you believe.

10. You've Had It All Along!

Remember, your purpose is not some magical, unattainable thing. It is something that is born into you. It's your gift to the world. It is the traits and habits inside of you that set you apart from others. There may be others with the same kind of traits, but there's no one else who has the same mixture of traits as you. Our purpose is to use those gifts and talents to better the communities in which we live.

11. Accept to Expect the Unexpected: How to Overcome Obstacles

It's not a matter of 'if' we will face obstacles, but rather a matter of 'when' we will face them. You cannot get away from obstacles. Something will, no doubt, throw a wrench in your plans. Instead of worrying about when that might happen or how it might happen, prepare for it to happen. How do you prepare to expect the unexpected? By simply accepting there will be things that come up. Allow some flexibility in your life and in your planning.

12. Determine What Motions to Go Through: Developing Habits for Success

Reaching your potential will be impossible without forming successful habits in your life. There are little things that will give you the edge over others in your market, such as waking up early, volunteering for the "less than" jobs, and simply showing up when others don't show up. Discipline should become one of your favorite words. Discipline shows you're taking charge of your time and deciding where it is spent, rather than allowing your time to rule you.

13. There Are Only So Many Hours in the Day: Understanding Moderation

Working out is great, but if you overdue it, you might pull a muscle. Learn to do things in moderation. There is a time to drink and a time to be sober. There is a time to work and a time to play. There is a time to hustle and there *MUST* be a time to rest!

14. Adulting: The Money Edition

Make sure you learn the basics about money. It doesn't grow on trees and it doesn't magically pay for your purchases every time you swipe a card. There has to be money available in the account that particular card represents. Learn how to budget, learn how to save, and learn how stay out of debt.

15. Make It to the Top – That'll Shut Them Up!

Hold on to that dream balloon. If others try to pop it, or actually do pop it, pull out the duct tape and show them what you got! Continue onward until you achieve your dream. Haters are always gonna hate. Instead of stopping in the middle of your race to argue with them, continue toward the finish line and win the medal. That'll shut them up.

16. Stop Looking for the Next Best Thing – Rock What You Got!

You are your brand. Be yourself. Focus on what you like and stick with it. If you're the only one in your town rocking Doc Martens, then own it! Carry your style, through everything that you do.

17. There Are Enough Haters in The World, Don't Be Your Own

Appreciate yourself. Stop putting yourself down, even if you're only joking around. If you joke around enough, you're eventually going to believe it. The world has enough haters, you don't need to be your own self-hater. Learn to love you.

18. Mirror, Mirror on The Wall I'm the Greatest One of All (maybe?)

Change your mindset. You are you—how can you be an imposter at that? It's time for you to stop taking every comment as negative and learn to move on with things. It's time to change your mindset to see the differences between failing and succeeding. Stop feeling like an imposter in your own life.

19. Start Making Your Money Work for You

Seek out others that are financially savvy. Develop plans and goals on how to spend your money to help you eliminate financial anxiety in your life.

Taking away all these lessons and combining them will help you reach your full potential. Just remember that reaching your full potential is not something you're magically going to achieve in one day. It's something you will be working toward and developing your whole life.

I'm sure, as soon as I finish this book, I'll start thinking, "Oh, maybe I should have added something about this." The list of things we need to know could continue on and on. Don't see these as the only things that twenty-somethings need to know, but rather as a foundation to build upon. Always seek to better yourself and what you know.

BONUS CHAPTER

Chapter 21

Your Beginning World Crisis – Coronavirus

"E Pluribus Unum"
Latin phrase translated, "Out of many, one."

As I was working to finish this book, the world as I know it, the world as *we* know it, seemed to get flipped upside down with one word—*coronavirus*. After developing a whole book about *20 Things 20-Somethings Need to Know*, I felt it was necessary to touch on a subject that had, quite literally, swept the world over.

We've never had a crisis that didn't involve the word "I" in the subject. We've had fears of war, global destruction, and environmental disasters, but we never imagined a faceless killer dropping us like flies. Has it changed us? Many of us were laid off (or we heard the wartime term "furloughed") and there were no gatherings on rooftop bars and no graduations, along with numerous other important events all being cancelled. It's no longer about the "I," but rather about the "us" and "we." *We* want to stay alive. *We* want our relatives to stay healthy. The ten minutes of deciding between passion pink or retro pink lipstick at Sephora were gone. So, who do we turn to for survival? The news? That helps for current situations and up-to-the-minute information, but what about the long-term future? Who understands our worries and our sanity?

Let's look back at previous generations—people in their seventies, eighties, nineties, and even the few 100-year-olds—who survived two World Wars, The Great Depression, and the 1918 Influenza Pandemic (erroneously called the Spanish flu) that infected 500 million people (25% of the world population) and killed as many as 100 million. What can we learn from all the survivors who made it through those difficulties?

I talked with renowned gerontologist Dr. Karl Pillemer, author of *"30 Lessons for Living"* and a professor at Cornell University. Dr. Pillemer has interviewed and studied older Americans and shares his knowledge through lectures and books. He suggests that Millennials and Gen Zers should take some time to talk to some older people around them from those time periods.

If you have the opportunity, go to your grandparents or great grandparents and ask them about the crisis they lived through.

"If there's one thing about older people—even
if you wouldn't go to them, necessarily, for advice
on how to reprogram the DVR or who the latest
reality star is one thing that older people
REALLY do have that younger people don't is
the knowledge of how to live through
hard times! Because they've done it!"
~ Dr. Karl Pillemer ~

Millennials and Gen Zers are anxious and we can't help it. Spreading anxiety is just what we do. So, how do younger people deal with anxiety in a crisis? What can we learn about dealing with anxiety from older people?

As we get older, we get better at regulating our emotions and looking at the longer view and the bigger picture. Well, that's really tough right now! Gen Zers have been proud of their recent accomplishments with not being as frivolous as Millennials and not having as much debt as Millennials. We've been braggers about not falling into Millennial mistakes in the world. Enter 2020 and Gen Zers start falling backward. The year 2020 has some of the oldest Gen Zers graduating college. But their schools are closed and classes are online-only, graduations have been canceled, jobs have been furloughed, and they have been quarantined for an undetermined amount of time.

Worrisome doesn't cover this type of avalanche. So, the first thing to address is your state of mind. How you respond will affect your future, so calm down and plan ahead. You're stepping into an economic recession. You're not the first to be in this position, but you want to survive and thrive through it. There are two important areas I'd suggest as a focus. First, keep your ears open to what the financial gurus are suggesting in order to start a good plan. Second, listen to those who have survived it during previous generations and respect how they survived it.

I discussed the novel coronavirus crisis with a financial expert:

Q: Tell me the vibe for Millennials and Gen Zers right now in regard to financial issues?

A: For those who prepared for a 3-6+ months cash reserve, it's a good time to buy into investments while the costs are low. If you weren't prepared for the 3-6 months cash reserve, then the ability to pay rent and other necessities is a bigger concern.

The CARES Act Stimulus Bill can help, as well as applying for unemployment, deferring existing loans like student loan payments, that will carry many through the next several months. "I think those who are the most uninformed, or lack critical information, are the most anxious at this point."

Q: If you're sitting at home during quarantine, what should you do? Actually, this goes for anything that has you sitting at home, whether it be the result of losing a job, a crisis, or an illness. How are we supposed to prepare for the future when everything is stagnant?

A: You need to act. Apply at your state's unemployment office for benefits. Contact your landlord to work out a deal on rent and go through your loan obligations to get them deferred. As for monies that you receive, such as the stimulus check through the CARES Act, take part of it and deposit into your savings account to help build a cash cushion.

Don't sit around worrying. Act and learn. There's a lot of online classes (many that are no cost to you from top colleges) where you'll be able to learn an additional trade, maybe even a new language. Or, if a person's had a hobby or side business they've been wanting to focus on previously, this is a great time to plan for it and get it set up.

So, for a lot of people, 2020 has been a wakeup call. There's been tremendous pain, like in all crisis situations. But keep a clear head, take warnings seriously, and plan your time. Your time, when you're stuck in isolation, shouldn't be unproductive. Have a goal to learn, to expand, and to experience self-growth and self-improvement during this time.

How can elderly people help? First, they lived through a crisis worse than yours. They just didn't have social media to promote it. We've got anxiety and plenty of it. Dr. Pillemer explains how older generations handled anxiety during a crisis.

1. Take the long view. Focus on the bigger picture, not the here and now and what's currently in your face.

2. Your behavior now is crucial. How we behave now is crucial. We need to be helpful, empathetic, and positive during the crisis. Then your story will be one you're proud to tell in the future.

3. Analyze how you view happiness. Millennials and Gen Zers go through life thinking happiness is achieved with the "if only." I'll be happy, if I get that great job or house. When you reach an older age—elderly people already know this—you'll realize you can be happy in spite of difficult things that happen to you along the way. Make a conscious decision to maximize happiness in your life. Older people have the philosophy of happiness as being a choice and not a condition. You have to actively work to make yourself happy!

4. Practice gratitude. Little things are things to be happy and satisfied about. A sunny day, your morning coffee, etc.

5. Worry is a double waste of time. Dr. Pillemer asked older Americans (seventy, eighty years old and older) what they regret? How can younger people prevent themselves from having regrets at an older age? The

number one thing? "I wish I hadn't spent so much time worrying!" was their answer! Worry wastes your life. Don't worry about things you have no control over.

6. Be generous. It's all about people helping people, because we are all in this together. And helping others makes you stronger and makes you feel better.

7. Stay connected. Utilize Facetime, Zoom, and whatever other ways you have to stay connected with people. We need to connect with others during this time. We should even connect with those from whom we have become estranged. At the end of the day, whatever the disagreement happened to be at that time, a crisis shows the estrangement was stupid. Solidarity and feelings of oneness are how previous generations got through a crisis.

8. Journal this, whether it's through videos or blogs, or actually writing in a paper journal. The moments will be preserved, as well as relieve you of what you're feeling.

9. Your new potential. How you look at the world will change. It'll be up to you, whether or not that change makes you stronger and wiser.

10. Get over how your life was before. The number one thing I see on all the social sites of friends is what they feel they're missing. I miss my friends, I miss my walks in the park, I miss... It's a new world that is coming into play and living in the past and reminiscing doesn't do anyone any good.

Bibliography

[1] https://www.readmoreco.com/blogs/authors-interviews/q-a-with-robert

[2] https://www.readmoreco.com/blogs/authors-interviews/q-a-with-robert

[3] https://psychology-spot.com/signs-that-someone-influences-your-life

[4] https://www.inc.com/melanie-curtin/why-millennials-feel-more-pressure-to-succeed-than-any-other-generation.html

[5] https://www.nytimes.com/2019/09/17/style/generation-z-millennials-work-life-balance.html

[6] https://www.weforum.org/agenda/2019/10/burnout-mental-health-pandemic/

[7] https://www.cnbc.com/2019/10/08/millennials-gen-z-have-quit-jobs-due-to-mental-health-issues-survey.html

[8] https://www.cnbc.com/2019/05/10/62-percent-of-millennials-say-they-are-living-paycheck-to-paycheck.html

[9] https://www.linkedin.com/pulse/49-millennials-struggle-imposter-syndrome-work-aimee-bateman/